I0758385

SOLITUDE SOLUTION
The Only Way Out

by Karen Kellock Ph.D.

FORMULA FOR THEORY:

ALL SUCCESS ATTRACTION
ALL DISEASE OBSTRUCTION
ALL RECOVERY ELIMINATION

The three obstructions are:
people, habit and food.

Remove your obstruction and
you snap to your goals,
waiting in the wings.

SOLITUDE SOLUTION

SOLITUDE is highest therapy. That means not just physical aloneness but social media avoidance.   It used to be you could erase an ex quick, but now with ease of internet stalking we just stay sick.   You're putting him first instead of yourself--always seeking *outer* validation by some louse. Move on and don't try to get back. The answer is solitude for it's not about them but the original trauma in childhood.

FRIENDS WRECK DESTINY

SEPARATION UNTO GOD
THE ANOINTING BREAKS BONDAGES
ISOLATION PREPARES FOR GREATER
FROM PIT TO PALACE
NOTICE HOW FAR YOU'VE COME
THE MIRACLE OF PRAYER
THE TERRIBLE DISEASES: ENVY/JEALOUSY
SATAN IS THE MOST JEALOUS
THE DEVIL'S MAD YOU MADE IT
REAL IS RARE/FAKE IS EVERYWHERE
CELEBRATE YOURSELF
YOUR ABSENCE KILLS EM
NEVER TAKE EM BACK
NEVER BEG FOR SUPPORT AGAIN
YOU SHOWED REAL AND GENUINE
NO MORE DIETING TO STAY THIN
BIG, RICH BREAKASTS THEN FAST

FRIENDS WRECK DESTINY

SEPARATION UNTO GOD

If God hadn't separated you'd never realize who you were in Christ. It's painful but that's the gist.

He had to get your undivided attention. He loved you so much He gave you a head start by separation.

Separation and isolation gives you the advantage. It's about your future and money you'll manage.

Your family, friends and exes can't go with you. They've all fallen behind: take a look at this Sue.

Through separation God molded you into the man or woman of God you're supposed to be too.

Now it all makes sense. You are the light surrounded by darkness and God removed that whole mess.

If you stayed enmeshed in that family you'd never become the godly He chose you to be.

THE ANOINTING BREAKS BONDAGES

The anointing in your life had no choice but to break those bondages: that is the whole message.

He couldn't get your attention with all the strongholds and hindering spirits that hid your merits.

Your past felt like a series of wars as He separated you from your peers: you had only your prayers.

Do you realize Satan tried to destroy you since a child? That God saved you from being defiled?

FRIENDS WRECK DESTINY

It was a sinful era: you swam in muddy waters but your God cut them all off, that's all that matters.

God separated you into the pit. You shook with horror as God did it, isolating you from ALL OF IT.

ISOLATION PREPARES FOR GREATER

ISOLATION is always preparing you for your greater. It feels like punishment but it's not sister.

What didn't kill you made you greater. God put you thru the furnace so you'd come out the master.

Separation gives you a head start for the new thing God is creating in you so look forward & stay cool.

The family who sold you out will watch you win from the balcony. Don't go back after treachery.

See where you're at right now: you're in your winning season. Look at what you had to go thru son.

God hid your value cuz He knew those around you were sent to destroy you. Count it all joy Sue.

It was sleep paralysis til God broke every chain. It was Satan holding you back from your calling ok.

FROM PIT TO PALACE

God had said "you may have to go thru this pit, but you'll end in the palace" and He kept that promise.

For years I ran away from God thru booze and pot but I escaped back cuz in His presence I felt awed.

God allowed me to go thru pain/torment to get my attention with my back against the wall son.

FRIENDS WRECK DESTINY

Jesus had to be separated from His disciples. He went into the wilderness separate from all peoples.

God said "don't ever go back to bondage, poverty, family--those who sold out. Now stay free."

You may have to lose everything to get sick & tired of the whole scene and come back to the clean.

As they were plotting and planning for my downfall God was planning my rising up after it all.

NOTICE HOW FAR YOU'VE COME

I can't believe how far I came. From being hated by the whole town to sitting in my mansion in fame.

God said if I held my peace & let Him fight my battles victory would be mine and it happened, aye.

People tend to pick on and bully the chosen one until one fateful day they have to fight back son.

Since God is freeing you, all you gotta do is hold your peace and you will win the victory too.

Painful separation hurts so much at first. You have no one to run to but God & it feels like a curse.

God said He would restore all those years taken from you. Your joy, strength and prosperity too.

Chosens are kind people. So don't confuse rejection with God's removal of someone due to evil.

Stop shrinking to fit dimwits and expand instead to fit the space their absence has left you with.

Relationships that seemed safe but were actually toxic will now disappear so feel bad or have fear.

FRIENDS WRECK DESTINY

Just as a lot needs to be cleared before something new built, deconstruct to reconstruct [be filled].

THE MIRACLE OF PRAYER

Prayer works! I can't believe how every little problem is solved just by asking the King first.

And there's always problems. Little one, big ones and doubts that need illumination and solvin'.

There seemed to be no solution to a malevolent woman who was buggin' but I woke up overcomin'.

God finds peculiar/unique answers to problems where there is no answer just by praying whenever.

All you did was grow & heal and people started hating. New level new devil, you gotta be expecting.

Weapons will form but they will not prosper. In the name of Jesus go on ahead, be a winner.

Jealousy is as cruel as the grave but your God gave you a way of escape so ignore it all and just pray.

I made it from rock bottom to the mountaintop so I see what you've been through: now don't stop.

People WILL fall away as you come up the ladder to fame. Don't fear it but just expect it, ok?

Start your youtube channel & express yourself how ever you want to and God will promote it too.

THE TERRIBLE DISEASES: ENVY/JEALOUSY

Jealousy and envy are terrible diseases. You gotta stay outa the way as you climb the ladder ok.

FRIENDS WRECK DESTINY

The bible says come out from amongst them. Separate from jealous spirits: you are the light son.

You're the center of attention without even trying, so stay out the way or be victim to conniving.

As good people we tend to go back to where God has brought us from but this never works son.

Just to prove a point or show off you tell bad spirits good news but you KNOW they're jealous of you!

When God gives you a way of escape you gotta STAY out of the way or be held back by envy.

SATAN IS THE MOST JEALOUS

Satan himself is the biggest jealous envious spirit and he's coming against you now, believe it.

You can't even date these days without em plotting and planning how to get what you have ok.

You can't even go around family without em jealously hating on you cuz you broke the mold Sue.

Here you wanna help them outa poverty but you gotta stay away cuz of their constant jealousy.

Your life is being re-arranged to accommodate blessings yet to come. So chin up, wait for em hon'.

God doesn't just cut the toxic but what doesn't serve or build you up kid. He readies you for your magic.

It's gonna be HUGE but you gotta stay out the way cuz those you help are so hatefully envious dude.

We're not wrestlin' against flesh & blood but spiritual wickedness in high places--not the neighborhood.

FRIENDS WRECK DESTINY

The only way to block their plottin' & plannin' is to ride alone cuz then you're with Jesus not a foe.

The minute you do better then them they'll start plottin' and plannin' how to ruin it for you man.

As hard as it is to be successful the lazy asses still have the nerve to feel they deserve it, not you.

THE DEVIL'S MAD YOU MADE IT

The devil's mad you made it outa the hood and poverty. He lost his chance cuz you're always busy.

You gotta keep moving. You can't go in certain environments now so what are you proving?

Toxic, jealous, envious spirits have now taken over the youth. They're killing people over very little too.

When God gives you a way out, stay out. After He plants your feet on higher ground, rid doubts.

Don't ever come back down to the enemy's level. You're on a high frequency, far above that devil.

REAL IS RARE/FAKE IS EVERYWHERE

Real is rare and fake is everywhere. It's very hard to find someone real so your absence scares.

Lovebombing would be great if it weren't ALWAYS followed by the discard, that's the narc.

Once they showed you who they were, you were gone. They can't sleep but it's a matter of survival now.

You're not coming back cuz jealousy is as cruel as the grave. You can't ever go back, it's too late.

FRIENDS WRECK DESTINY

You gave til you couldn't take it anymore. They saw you as the problem but you were their savior.

Once they returned your gift and treated you like shit it was just too late and you ghosted em ok.

CELEBRATE YOURSELF

Now you're in a season of celebrating yourself. You'd never go back to ingrates jealous as hell.

They'd **NEVER** do for you what you did for them. They'd sell you out in a minute, take if from me friend.

The minute you start celebrating yourself you'll attract the right kind of people, escaping this hell.

You carried the essence of God but they did you wrong. You're a rare gem and now they can't get along.

They used you, stealing finances and your energy. You're tired & will do your own thing, finally.

If people aren't giving you the same energy you're giving to them, from now on you gotta ghost again.

Jealousy is everywhere so you gotta guard your spirit, you're rare. Lay low, don't boast, use prayer.

Your absence is speaking volumes now. But now that you know that get on with it: earn, grow.

YOUR ABSENCE KILLS EM

Trust me, your absence is being felt right now. A rare gem isn't easily forgotten but **WATCH OUT**.

They had the nerve to discard/ghost you first when you didn't do anything to deserve their curse.

FRIENDS WRECK DESTINY

Now you're gonna ghost people like they ghosted you. You're gonna do it first, a Ph.D. in ghosting sir.

People come and go and you're not a people-addict like those fellows. It's God who is King you know.

NEVER TAKE EM BACK

Now that you're gone they want you back. They feel like they can't live without you, that's a fact.

But they'll do it again, that's the dam human element. You've gotta be solitary now to make a mint.

When you ghost em they're gonna feel it. Once that new supply stops working you can expect it.

You cannot refriend someone who tried to destroy you but are now terrified of what they lost too.

A chosen can't get back into old relationships when that last moment was so hectic, treacherous, tragic.

Why would it never work out? Because you guys are not on one accord. They proved that and more.

You're not together in the spiritual realm. You're one with God, they're believing in the world, awed.

NEVER BEG FOR SUPPORT AGAIN

You can never beg for their support and help again. You need those who want to without thinkin'.

First class treatment should come automatically, not you beggin' for it like you've been doin' lately.

Some of you have wasted years so why would you take em back, to waste more ending in tears?

FRIENDS WRECK DESTINY

When they show you who they are, BELIEVE em. Now they're crying in their beer but ignore it man.

YOU SHOWED REAL AND GENUINE

You showed em you were real, genuine and that you had their back. And they STILL did all that: fact!

They deliberately mistreated you because you belong to God. That isn't changed, you saw the flawed.

They shunned you for being blessed and highly favored. They turned their back cuz you're anointed sir.

Your absence is their misery right now. Too late, let em go thru it for you're going to the next level.

They're filled with confusion because you were the peacemaker and now you're gone forever.

You carried the peace of God surpassing all understanding, which the bullies are now craving.

You gave them so many chances, you know you did. But until you were gone they gave you shit.

They actually took your kindness as a weakness, a joke! That happened til now, released from their yoke.

They thought you'd always put up with their mess, being a yes-person so weaselly in your weakness.

NO MORE DIETING TO STAY THIN

I've ended on high-fat: don't wanna be stuffed with starch or veg and forget fruit for my ONE meal.

I felt so starchy living on starch, blocked up. Veggies are ok but I love salsa for my main antioxidant.

FRIENDS WRECK DESTINY

Just not into fruit except on hot days. Don't crave the sweet so sorry Freelee, can't live that way.

Cheese collapses calories so don't have to stuff much before my 24 hr fast. It's efficient I attest.

So glad to get off the starch diet. Corn, potatoes, beans are fine once in awhile but not a constant.

Not into meat or eggs. Fish once in awhile but don't crave it. Just cheese dishes then get on with it.

Neither veggies nor fruit suffice for one meal a day. Starches do but feels like a pillow I ate.

Lost three pounds on two days of cheese meal. Can't help it I like being skinny with so much zeal.

I lost three pounds by switching from starches to fats--the opposite to what you'd think about that.

BIG, RICH BREAKASTS THEN FAST

I've finally said: "frig all diets". The French are thin and they combine it all: starches, sugars and fats.

I had French toast this morning: eggs, milk, bread, butter and maple syrup like I did as a kid.

I feel GREAT: like I did at a young age. I fueled the tank with a rich breakfast then fasted/worked all day.

The issue is ONE MEAL A DAY [OMAD]. Eat whatever you want and FORGET DIETING, that's that.

All restriction gave me acid reflux later. With a rich breakfast I feel so even, SO much better.

The French toast was dripping with butter--so what? And the maple syrup gave me energy, a LOT.

FRIENDS WRECK DESTINY

Eating only starch on the Starch Solution made me feel bready and starchy, full and very lazy.

I've been a dieter [restrictor] since ten. It's time to come back to roots [big/rich breakfasts only], amen.

The Scotch are known for huge breakfasts. Never knowing when they'd eat again that was it.

SEPARATION AND ISOLATION

YOUR TRIALS ARE PROOF
EVERY SCAR EQUIPS PEOPLE
THE HELL YOU WENT THRU EQUIPT YOU
WE'VE ALL SINNED, FORGET IT ALL
BLOCKED COMING TO THE NEXT LEVEL
SELF-HATE COMING TO SUCCESS
HINDERING SPIRITS BEING CLOSE
LONELINESS IS JUST SEPARATION
SIGNS OF BREAKTHROUGH: LONELY TOO
BOUNDARIES FORCE SEPARATION
YOUR ENTRY IS UPON THEIR EXIT
THRILLED THEN REJECTED, SO WHAT
WORK, SHUT EM OUT, RELAX
CHOSENS: REGRETS TURN TO ASSETS
FROM OVERLOOKED TO YOUR GOOD
THE ANOINTING DESTROYS YOKES

SEPARATION AND ISOLATION

YOUR TRIALS ARE PROOF

Your trials--so tribulative--are **PROOF** God has chosen you. They prepared you for greatest war Sue.

Thru the fire of suffering you emerge not broken but transformed thru the furnace of affliction.

The refining process wasn't easy, it stripped you of everything that held you back completely.

Now you stand on the other side, not a victim of circumstance but a **HEALER** of all, aye.

Joseph went from the worst family betrayal and slavery to save millions from a killing famine see.

Unimaginable hardship makes people vessels of God's healing and redemption: true leadership son.

The weaker are still broken and seeking hope: those are the ones you'll be helping, able to cope.

EVERY SCAR EQUIPS PEOPLE

Every scar you carry/tear you shed has power to equip people in the midst of terrible trouble and evil.

You would not have this tremendous power had you not gone through those tribulations so dire.

Troubles & strife: God put you through **HELL** to fulfill the extraordinary purpose He put on your life.

Being put through hell so you could save the world: what a way to deal with bad memories girl.

SEPARATION AND ISOLATION

A "divine" healer's been transformed through the darkest valleys with the power to heal everybody.

A divine healer has the power to RENEW people, those who've lost all hope after victimized by evil.

Your deepest wounds will be used as divine instruments of healing: what a way to deal with memories!

THE HELL YOU WENT THRU EQUIPT YOU

The hell you went thru was the only way God could equip you for the high calling you had Sue.

Imagine a woman escaping the torment of an abusive marriage: aging quickly/feeling discouraged.

She takes the strength to rebuild her life then takes it to fulfill her purpose: in all realms that's how it works.

When the holy spirit's backing you there's nothing the foe can do. It's a sealed deal until through.

You've been thru hell but it's rewarded by lives you save and all the perks coming to you as well.

God is molding and shaping you from all you've been thru. The power of this anointing is incredible.

WE'VE ALL SINNED, FORGET IT ALL

We've all sinned and fallen short of the glory of God. Just pick yourself up again and forget it all.

Ain't it funny how just when you get so close negative thoughts come in your mind the most?

Just when close you recall embarrassing moments or think "I am nothing" or "I deserve opponents".

SEPARATION AND ISOLATION

Ask God to take every negative thought into captivity. That's how you handle demonic entities.

It's not just attacks from others but an inner critic. You feel worthless, over the hill, even a lunatic.

People and thoughts will be lashing out at you when you're SO CLOSE to that breakthrough too.

You start to think your work is worthless right when it's about to be recognized as priceless.

Remember this too: It's WHEN you're close to breakthrough that Satan tries to distract you.

BLOCKED COMING TO THE NEXT LEVEL

Just when you try for the next level here comes something to block you or cause trouble.

Take hindering spirits as a SIGN: that's the way to handle this frustrating pattern as old as time.

When chums came around you weren't strong enough to resist fiery darts from your home town.

Trying to fit in makes you easily influenced. This eclipses your whole personality like a dunce.

God said "what are you doing, I called you to LEAD." But He didn't rush me, I had to go thru it see.

SELF-HATE COMING TO SUCCESS

It's good to know when you're closest to success you'll feel most negative about yourself I guess.

You gotta remember everything coming THRU you was from God cuz you're pure now [tho' flawed].

SEPARATION AND ISOLATION

You're God's: You meekly compare yourself to famous movie producers but that's not the point sir.

When nothing's happening it's easy to feel God forgot about you but it means the opposite Sue.

Satan knows he can't stop the anointing so he sends evil entities for your self-deprecating.

You feel "it's all over, I'm done for"--that's his plan, just when your breakthrough's around the bend.

HINDERING SPIRITS BEING CLOSE

Now that your close, here comes all these hindering spirits. When you think of this it makes sense.

Satan makes you wanna throw in the towel just before God wants to bring in your great destiny now.

Say "I shall receive my breakthru and all God has promised me". Then recall: don't get weary.

You are getting ready to reap IF you faint not. It's like this at the end, always recall this thought.

If God is for you, no devil in hell or anyone you know can be against you. Remember this always Sue.

It's when nothing's happening that we question ourselves. Ask God to remove this demonic spell.

LONELINESS IS JUST SEPARATION

Loneliness and nothingness is actually just separation which is for your advantage in the interim.

You're making your ENTRY upon their EXIT. Thus it feels like nothingness when you're about to make it.

SEPARATION AND ISOLATION

No matter how lonely you feel, don't go back into bondage. That's what it is with the foolish.

God's broken the chains off of you to be free, but it feels like a hideous situation being all alone see.

God's not punishing but preparing you for your greater. Letting go of dead weights is the way there.

You were the one in your family who got sold out, because you were chosen before birth by God.

SIGNS OF BREAKTHROUGH: LONELY TOO

Always remember this about breakthrough: in the end the more lonely you feel the more it is true.

The more you're rejected by people or publishers, the more it's true you're God's sons/daughters.

You didn't understand why God had to separate you from friends: why they dumped you then.

Twits: Cuz God chose you before the foundation of this world, you make your entry upon their EXIT.

They want to drop in whenever they want because they're "family" but you don't like the interrupt

You put boundaries on them: "visit only on Sundays". They think you should welcome them always.

BOUNDARIES FORCE SEPARATION

Boundaries alone are enough to force separation from the narcissistic throng: you can't get along.

It doesn't matter who it is: you hate surprise or interruption and that's the whole point son.

SEPARATION AND ISOLATION

They wanna drop in but you put boundaries up and that's all that's needed to stop this stuff.

I was finally free when I put a boundary on thee but it pissed you off because you're a narcissist see.

I laid my burdens down when i said "don't come around" cuz you went away in a huff with ego put down.

The religious narcissist is a manipulator too: "the holy spirit told me to drop in to pray for you".

YOUR ENTRY IS UPON THEIR EXIT

Your entry is upon their exit, so don't be depressed or anxious one bit when all alone for a minute.

They say they wanna work with you then go away. Choose your team very carefully & be happy.

You can't stand interruptions or surprises and that includes "family" but they can't stand this.

If it's just ONE on your team it's ok so ignore the traitors who go away you didn't need em anyway.

God promised you breakthrough and prosperity, that's all you need to know in these last days.

You were the best on their team but got fired anyway. Again, your ENTRY is upon their EXIT ok?

THRILLED THEN REJECTED, SO WHAT

They were "thrilled" by your colab but then something turned them off suddenly: who cares honey?

Do your work with devotion, watch movies/listen to music for recreation then ignore all of em.

SEPARATION AND ISOLATION

Be happy you have ONE companion [as God said you'd always have one] and enjoy what's left son.

God called you to do a great thing with your life chosen ones. No worries, breakthrough will come.

This separation & isolation you're in right now will save your life so don't see it any other way, aye.

So you're tottering on your last legs: that's all you need to get over the finish line/surpass the dregs.

WORK, SHUT EM OUT, RELAX

Work, shut them out, rest. Work, shut them out, relax. Work, shut them out, recreate to be best.

So they fired you. You weren't supposed to be with them anyway tho' they looked so good Sue.

Eyes have not seen/ears have not heard the plans God has in store for you, so hold on & stay true.

His plan is to give you a hope and a future, an expected END. Hold on to this promise and never give in.

You've been separated since you were a child, this is nothing new. You were an outcast in school!

You would NEVER fit in cuz God hand-picked you--He CHOSE you! That means alone, not blue.

The majority of you chosens have been through poverty--financial and emotional--with their family.

CHOSENS: REGRETS TURN TO ASSETS

Chosens have been thru generational curses, deaths & regrets but no sweat they turned into assets.

SEPARATION AND ISOLATION

Your painful separation is to your advantage: getting to the promised land despite all the damage.

Due to this separation you're getting a head start to your breakthrough and all the perks that accrue.

All the torment and sleepless nights during isolation will go for your greater-- just around the corner.

FROM OVERLOOKED TO YOUR GOOD

You feel alone, rejected and overlooked but I promise you chosen it'll all work out for your good.

You didn't need that colab anyway. He was just a fly by night, an empty case tho' a handsome face.

All you need now is to persevere & dry your tears. Look forward to breakthrough and have no fears.

You may feel alone but you're not alone. God never leaves nor forsake you, He's here in your home.

I never understood when God separated me from family. It wasn't until years later I saw His plan fully.

The majority of my life I had chains holding me down. Those people were a hindrance all around.

God had no choice but to separate me from my system. My family, hometown, old friends--all of em.

THE ANOINTING DESTROYS YOKES

Because I had an anointing over my life it destroyed the yokes of bondage: PEOPLE, that's my message.

I honestly felt God forgot about me. Until I learned to hold on to scriptures of His holy promises see.

SEPARATION AND ISOLATION

They're mad you didn't have to be blessed by their approval. They're not God ya' know Sue.

If you're in God's favor the whole world can be against you and He'll still be for you: take that view.

When their tactics don't work to hold you down they'll get sick to get your sympathy or the town's.

PLIGHT OF THE CHOSEN
SEPARATE MEANS HOLY

THE CROWD MAKES EM NERVOUS
HIDDEN UNDER GOD'S HAND
DISRESPECT TRIGGERS
ADDICTIVE TRAPS: BULIMIA
REPENT FOR BOLD ESCAPE
PARENTS: INOCULATE YOUR KIDS!
NEVER SETTLE MYRTLE
TRANSCEND THE JEALOUS
CHOSEN CAN BE NO FUN
HOME IS EVERYTHING
SELF-DESTRUCTIVE AGEIST
ISOLATION MAKES YOU PROLIFIC
THE RAGING WOUNDED NARCISSIST
BURNING CHEST/RACING HEART
MY END THOUGHTS

PLIGHT OF THE CHOSEN
SEPARATE MEANS HOLY

The scriptures say in the last days your enemies will be your own family members see--really.

They passed you by and discarded you like an old shoe when lured by new supply but you survived.

THE CROWD MAKES EM NERVOUS

They're uncomfortable in your presence. They don't think "it's a highly conscious being" but a nuisance.

They feel uncomfortable with your strong presence and energy but mostly: they don't know why see.

Since you trigger undefined emotions in them they instantly see you as the problem friend.

By the time you're old trauma created a startle response meaning socializing makes you nervous.

I just like being alone in my own wonderful world with my pets and a big window of nature here.

The best is a marriage of two saints who protect each other's solitude so they can be alone too.

Everything changed being married. I rarely saw him but I came behind a wall and that was for me, ALL.

To be ignored, scorned, a stranger in a strange land then married/loved is so wonderful man.

You're now one unit who forges all the crap together. It makes all the difference in life or whatever.

PLIGHT OF THE CHOSEN

HIDDEN UNDER GOD'S HAND

Did God lift His hand on your birthday? If He did better get ready cuz it'll be like a Tsunami ok.

You've been hidden under God's hand for years or decades, preparing for the big day when aged.

You thought you were just unpopular or a loser, all cuz you've been isolated in a bubble sir.

You've had to be alone. Being with others was a loud cacophonous siren and you longed for home.

In the world you were compared to inferiors and easily replaced as if your gifts were irrelevant sir.

Don't stay in a bad situation because you could have it worse or are afraid of being lonely, a curse.

I saw women submissive/passive right away. He didn't earn their respect, they were just a lay.

Today men want women to work just like them. So why the passive crap before you know him?

Women play wifey right away. Here he's breaking her down daily and she gets more submissive ok.

DISRESPECT TRIGGERS

Too many women are miserable in their situation having allowed men to take ALL of their power son.

Most times she doesn't have a REAL commitment and gives all her power away anyway to men.

I used to be sheepish thinking they'd love me more. A sweet lil' lady: but not for these jokers.

PLIGHT OF THE CHOSEN

Men won't respect it and take everything you have little lady dumb-lit. You want equal relationship.

Don't "help" a man or lend money to him. You don't want a gigolo you want a real alpha man.

He urges you to "take his lead" but wants you to work as hard as him Sue and be his sex slave too.

This is all cuz you didn't have a dad to instruct you about men. In the old days that never happened.

He KNOWS how to respect someone, he just doesn't respect YOU and it's quite evident Sue.

People act differently according to context: it's clear to everyone in the room when there's disrespect.

ADDICTIVE TRAPS: BULIMIA

She hears these signs and it triggers dis-ease subconsciously but she denies it all see.

A young girl discerns/feels disrespect and falls into bulimia or other addictive traps to absorb it.

Food means MOTHER and without the skill set to deal with disrespect she naturally falls into it.

We can't fall down in response to disrespect but STAND UP to it, only possible only thru repentance.

Sinful traps only weaken us making us miss the mark more as relationship goes toxic to the core.

To resolve relational problems the ONLY winning solution is repentance, I can really see this.

We can't fall down in response to disrespect but STAND UP to it which is only possible thru repentance.

PLIGHT OF THE CHOSEN

REPENT FOR BOLD ESCAPE

Repentance brings necessary boldness which is lacking in sinful weak vessels caving in to compliance.

If you're better than you've ever been, WHY would you want to go back/be young again friend?

If you can finally get back your OWN POWER you will manifest the new wonderful life you desire.

I don't want to go back even ten years. Everything was necessary climbing a latter based on tears.

PARENTS: INOCULATE YOUR KIDS!

Before you learn about people you're gonna have to suffer and those lessons are real bummers.

My parents never warned me about people. Mom just said to be a good hostess not to be careful.

Dad never educated me about men: that's they'd use me if I didn't hold my head up high/fence in.

People worship is our biggest block. Trying to get their approval is a form of this and it really sux.

You give in to a man, invite him in as slaver. A year later he'll find a really nice woman and marry her.

Sexual liberation did nothing but enslave women. Sluts have no power & many hearts are broken.

Women have no power except withholding and that's how it's been from the beginning darling.

Why SHOULD she give him sexual favors if he's mistreating her the rest of the day sir?

NEVER SETTLE MYRTLE

PLIGHT OF THE CHOSEN

Never settle Myrtle! Find a man who loves and never disrespects you and life will be fertile.

The genders do **NOT** have equal sex desire and to say they do puts women down with no power.

Her power comes from **DIGNITY** not laying down for a man who wants sex **ALL THE TIME** see.

When a man is jealous cuz you have more than he has it'll be rough as he cuts you down to death.

You can tell he's jealous by how he treats you. Envy is a deadly sin and low vibration: it gets cruel.

Having detected envy you don't wanna be around them cuz it'll affect your energy--that's it honey.

TRANSCEND THE JEALOUS

Transcend the jealous/envious people who just wanna bring you back down to where they are, evil.

I too was held down by their lowness your highness. I too wasted years adapting to losers sis.

The problem is after going separate they live in your head. All the time, what you shoulda said.

Your solitude and isolation was an incubator for leadership. Protected while getting fit.

Being with people was torture. They misjudged me, were suspicious, even despised me for sure.

Finally after several lonely years I met a man who I could easily talk to and married him right away too.

A kindred spirit, someone who understood me and I felt comfortable with, no misjudgments: YES!

PLIGHT OF THE CHOSEN

Until that moment I was a stranger in a strange land but with marriage all became positive and grand.

CHOSEN CAN BE NO FUN

Those who hold such a radiant light create both positive and negative reactions in others, aye.

I don't ask God how to make money, I do what He tells me to do knowing He wants to prosper me.

Chosen ones are so different they're also misunderstood by family, ever hear of it?

Some will want what you have and track you down, some will hate your guts/kill you for fun.

You can maximally enjoy your latter days if you've found your limitations and work within them ok.

I took extreme chances with my health when young, now I'm so careful and always stay at home.

HOME IS EVERYTHING

What's lovely about being older is STAYING HOME. An intense appreciation for one's unique abode.

Not trying to get approval anymore or getting sore. Just love around of animals and angels, to soar!

HOME: That's what it's all about. Where you walk tall and totally yourself without social thoughts.

To be home is to be in eternity. To be fighting with humans puts us back in dry boring temporality.

Like escaping to a cabin and feeling relief from the energy thief, that's how every day should be.

PLIGHT OF THE CHOSEN

No more games, fames, mixed signals, petty competitions or Jezebels: we're outa that hell.

You wanna be forty again in an office with the jealous broads or here--NOW--in your lovely abode?

All I need is a table to eat, work and sleep on and some shelves to keep order, that's all hon'.

Retirement is like putting on cozy pajamas and relaxing on an unplanned day of play like a Saturday.

Before relocating people used to drop by. I adapted to this until realizing I'd become their slave, aye.

People are bored/lonely & I'm never bored/lonely so they drove me crazy but now I'm so happy.

SELF-DESTRUCTIVE AGEIST

Are you 75 and filled with declining fears or looking ahead to blissful retirement for 25 years?

You are 75 and mother died at 76 so your fearful mind creates your death: that's how it works.

With such down-putting messages on aging from the media, being weaker the elder mimics it.

I lived in the desert wilderness for 31 years, apart from society and alone. That slowed aging down.

With no man to protect me it was scary and sad but still I didn't age as if in a phony social crowd.

ISOLATION MAKES YOU PROLIFIC

Isolation made me prolific cuz all my energy went towards that not exhausting human crap.

PLIGHT OF THE CHOSEN

One-upmanship, brinksmanship. resource guarding, scapegoating: all of it ages us the fastest.

Most exhausting is endlessly explaining ourselves cuz they don't understand us or are suspicious.

They're not empathic, kind gals/guys. They'll kick you to the curb when getting the upper hand, always.

They suicide to avoid old age when here it's the highest stage, one earned from years of tears/rage.

She seemed nice enough but getting a leg up she became a raging thief who cleaned me out.

THE RAGING WOUNDED NARCISSIST

How to maintain my edge became my entire purpose since if not I'd lose in a bedlam/insane circus.

They'r too weak to stay high and strong, they always regress to the devil's throne/doing wrong.

The wicked bands are sticky. You almost have to relocate for a restraining order gets tricky.

The wicked are vindictive, not above hiring a hit on the good who just wants freedom from twits.

The raging wounded narcissist is not about to let you go so easily, it's just a reality of who he is see.

Never tell him of your escape plans or threaten him. Stay silent til the end: it's survival friend.

Have GOOD recall: The elect have a history of very close calls and God rescuing them from them all.

It's all great here. I'm away from haters, toxic miserable family reminders and mentally I'm so clear.

PLIGHT OF THE CHOSEN

You can't trust anyone these days let alone your blood relatives--sounds like an awful thing to say?

The hateful blood relatives don't want you to get ahead of them in life: the truth hurts good, aye.

God has given us the KEYS: cut these miserable people off and stop giving them any time at all.

BURNING CHEST/RACING HEART

I'll take ONE chocolate covered almond a day after lunch ok. Now we'll see if it's all about restraint.

One chocolate covered almond, ok. But two: theobromine poisoning and nervous hell to pay.

It takes 18 days to get cacao [theobromine] out of the system. This is getting scarier by the day man.

Couldn't believe it when I read it: 3 things causing heart palpitations are coffee, alcohol, chocolate.

And heart palps always go with ACID REFLUX so I've no desire for alcohol, coffee or chocolates.

Coffee, alcohol and chocolates are the drugs of this world and they made me a very sick girl.

A racing heart right next to chest pains/acid reflux: is this not a pandemic reaction which sux?

A mild diet eaten mid-day with no dinner since that brings choking in your sleep in latter days.

I found my line: one chocolate covered almond and not one lick past that or i'm up crazy creek, aye.

Chocolate is more like a rattlesnake than pot. One cacao covered nut and I'm off on a toot.

PLIGHT OF THE CHOSEN

One chocolate covered nut in a 100 lb woman is enough to elevate [fly out the window], I mean it man.

With age you think with strange pains: is this the day? It throws an entirely different light on things ok.

All he needs is a roof, a couch, a bed and a television along with his frig & grill by George Foreman.

MY END THOUGHTS

The "odor of mendacity" means perjury which is a felony and it was to get President Donald Trump see.

On your project you're forced on a tangent. See it as part of the trip tho' you didn't plan on it.

You reach a point of inevitable success and just gliding. You're going with the flow, not doing anything.

Mass homelessness: This is really happening and it's sobering. The cold, heat, wet: I. can't imagine.

I had canyons in my life [living in a cabin surrounded by strife] but never without a roof or bed, aye.

Extend your husband's life by setting the tone then leaving him alone. Bring order then be gone.

The more ignored you were the more mass attractions are sure to occur. All you gotta do is: prepare.

What makes me love him is how he gives me privacy. I hardly know him but that's all I need see.

A female writer achieves success exhausted. After going thru all the above she's earned it.

It' a peculiar situation son. I had to write a new theory in psychology or be seen as an aberration.

CONTAGION OF MADNESS

THE NARCISSISTIC DISCARD
HE SEES WOMEN AS INTERCHANGEABLE
THEY ACT LIKE THEY OWN YOU
ATTACHED TO WEEDS CHOKING YOU
INTERMITTENT VALIDATION
NARCISSISTS FALL INTO THEIR OWN TRAP
THE CONTAGION OF MADNESS
MASS PSYCHOSES
VEGAN HYPNOTIC BLUES
GLOBALISTS KNOW WE NEED RED MEAT
LATEST WORDS

CONTAGION OF MADNESS

THE NARCISSISTIC DISCARD

This nightmare taught you about narcissism and the throng but God won't let you suffer for long.

It was a terrible experience discarded like trash but the lessons from it will shoot you ahead, promise.

Hide your love of pets from the narcissist cuz when he gets rages they may be the recipients.

HE SEES WOMEN AS INTERCHANGEABLE

He sees women as interchangeable: that oughta really piss you off. Avoid him/show him who's boss.

You sense your identity of interchangeability with this guy. Like you're nothing special at all, aye.

Being so dispensable that's enough reason to drop the pill. It's sickening Mabel, get a grip Ethel.

He'll drop you and go to another. It's a subtle threat for you to keep your act together Heather.

She must abandon her pets so they can get a pet together. No empathy, he's a real bummer.

THEY ACT LIKE THEY OWN YOU

He felt like he owned you just cuz he wanted you. That's the modern bedlam/tear down Sue.

He doesn't deserve you so don't degrade yourself. The corny/filthy world's values are not yours elf.

CONTAGION OF MADNESS

Narcissists block the sun outa your life and full potential. It's the wheat from tares I betcha.

Learn about the narcissist to see why you shouldn't want him. Surely victory is close then.

Get out at harvest--separating weeds--or stay attached to what's taking your nutrients see.

ATTACHED TO WEEDS CHOKING YOU

Stay attached to weeds in your life, who will continue to choke you out and blind your eyes?

You'll never be effective and live out your purpose with the weeds in your life: sucking spirits.

Harvest is a time of separation--from these weeds in your life. Of course you don't want to, aye.

The wheat and tares are separated at harvest. They grow up together to show their differences.

NEVER let the narcissist know everything you know about him. Just have wisdom, shrewdly movin'

His insufferable arrogance [dripping with conceit & grandiose utterance] brought my final exit.

A charming and captivating personality can make it difficult to recognize his harmful toxicity.

INTERMITTENT VALIDATION
 the hardest to release

Thru intermittent validation you're pulled into a trauma bond that never ends: rejection/come again.

Inconsistent validation: an abusive cycle like none other. Come here/go away/she's prettier.

CONTAGION OF MADNESS

You're being primed to seek validation while fearing a negative outcome: it's a hamster wheel son.

NARCISSISTS FALL INTO THEIR OWN TRAP

A narcissist can't help but fall into his own trap cuz he's compelled to fail promoting such crap.

Make believe God'll give you a million each time you don't go back and soon prosperity's a fact.

What a miserable day hating past and worrying future when it coulda been so much better.

Infection: When around him your ideas about self change, are distorted--self-worth aborted.

Because you'll do anything it takes to get the job done you chase everyone away for good hon'.

Stop talking about who didn't protect you. You gotta do that yourself--stop relying on "friends" too.

The parent's emotional state affects the brain development of the child who then goes wild.

The lack of transitional forms proves evolution to be untrue. There are **NONE** said me to fools.

To cure heartbreak simply get into your own life in marvelous detail. See? It's so dam cool.

THE CONTAGION OF MADNESS

The masses never seek truth. They turn away from facts and glorify error if they are seduced.

Whoever supplies with delusions becomes master, whoever discounts em becomes the foe sir.

CONTAGION OF MADNESS

There are times in history when mental illness is the norm not the exception: we're here son.

There is no protection from psychic epidemics when everyone's mad yet no one questions it.

Mental epidemics cause more harm than earthquakes or any other natural catastrophes around.

MASS PSYCHOSES

The bible speaks of rude, monstrous and debauched generations of the race: murder, orgies, rape.

The witches were scapegoats when groupies went mad and eventually there were no women left.

The madmen in the matrix become inferior morally: the society "sinks" into a hellish pit eventually.

The intellectual level sinks: they become unreasonable, emotional, irresponsible and erratic finks.

It's too easy to text a man--she's chasing you! She did it thrice yesterday: not a lady but a fool.

VEGAN HYPNOTIC BLUES

Protein deficiency shows as decreased immunity, swelling, horrible skin, fatigue and irritability.

To cure all skin problems simply substitute animal protein and fat for all your little snacks.

Dry patches, lines, wrinkles and ugly splitting come from protein deprivation not with plenty.

As an ex-vegan I could not eat the animal on the plate but having matured I could, changing my fate.

CONTAGION OF MADNESS

Extreme orthorexia from Ehretism and veganism ruined the body but animal fat brought me back.

Paleo scientists show we need the fat even more than protein for energy, balance, mental, sheen.

I may wanna carb up in the morning but the rest of the day it's protein-only because I've studied.

GLOBALISTS KNOW WE NEED RED MEAT

Globalists know we need red meat so put it down in the sixties and wanna kill all the cows see.

Breakfast: ice cream [does the trick]. Capsules: fruit/veggie, beets, collagen, vit. B--now MEAT.

It's just gonna be dairy and meat for awhile plus my superfood capsules: it's a new reality guys.

If your skin looks that way just imagine your insides, aye. Maybe God gave it to us as a sign.

Wrinkles: they're not from AGE but from non-replacement of increasing protein needs AS we age.

You must increase your protein intake with age or you will certainly look your age or worse ok.

LATEST WORDS

When God instructs, do it though it makes no sense. It's a perfect hit cuz God plays 12 D chess.

If it's small talk shut up and if it's important say it but nip it in the bud: I'm busy so I'm abrupt.

SOLITUDE SOLUTION
The Only Way Out

CULTURAL THRESHOLD LEVELS
SUSPECT FOR BEING DIFFERENT
AMBULANCE CHASER
DEVIL BRINGS SHAME TO THOUGHTS
HOLOCAUST DENIERS ARE COMPLAINERS
ESCAPE INTO SOLITUDE [YOU]
SOCIAL PSYCHOLOGY IS FASCINATING
THE POTTER'S WHEEL
ONCE IT'S OVER LET IT STAY OVER
GOD SHOWS AT LAST MINUTE
REPENT YE [THEN GO ON]
THE CHILDREN OF MISFORTUNE
WHAT MAKES EM IGNORANT?
GUILT AND SHAME REPEATS
STAND UP FOR SOLITUDE/PRIVACY
THE NICE IMAGE OF CONTROLLERS
MOST WOMEN WATCH CNN
THE WHOLE WORLD IS EVIL
MEMORY IS THE DEVIL'S TOOL
AGEIST COMMENTS
GOOD IS BAD AND BAD IS GOOD
HOOKED TO REJECTION CHEMICALS
EMOTIONAL DEPLETION
STOP NEEDING THE OUTER WORLD
OBSESSIONS FROM EARLY TRAUMAS
HIS COLDNESS TRIGGERS TERROR
EXPECT HIS/HER PUNISHMENTS
ONLY ONE, THE REST SHUN
BE A SELF-PARTNER
REACTION IN SEXUAL AFFAIRS
RISE ABOVE AS THE NEW BRASS

SOLITUDE SOLUTION

The Only Way Out

UTTER CRUELTY IS ALL OK-ED
TOUGH LOVE IS JUST BEING MEAN
FEMINISM IS SPLITTING FAMILIES
MOST EVIL IS SOCIAL HYPNOTISM
STAY HIGHNESS NO MATTER WHAT
INFLUENCE FEMININE OR FEMINIST?
FEMALE ACCUSATIONS AND ADDICTIONS
DUMMY GENERATION BY DESIGN
PEOPLE ARE TRIBAL: UNTRUE
STEERING PUBLIC OPINION WITH ILLOGIC
SAINTS ARE MILD AND SOBER
AT SOME POINT YOU LET IT ALL GO
THE TOLERANT ARE MOST INTOLERANT
MOST PEOPLE DON'T STUDY
MEN: PLEASE STOP APOLOGIZING
EVERYTHING REFLECTS *HER*
YOU'RE TOO SENSITIVE FOR THIS WORLD
FAKE PREACHERS ARE MILQUETOAST
GANG MENTALITY TRIFLES IN CYCLES
PULL THE PLUG ON MIND-CLUTTER
HELL: LIVING WITH FEMINIST SLOGANS
COLOR IS JUST A DIVISIVE TACTIC
LIBERALS HATE OUR CONFIDENCE
OBVIOUS: DEMOCRATS HAVE NO MORALS
RETURNING FROM THE BRINK
FIGHT EVIL OR FIGHT STATUES?
THE "VIEW" INTIMIDATES AS A GROUP
LIBERALS AND THEIR MAKE BELIEVE WORLD
PURITANS BROUGHT ORDER AND DISCIPLINE
LIBERAL CONFORMISTS CONDONE IT ALL
FREEDOM-LOVING IS HOME-LOVING

SOLITUDE SOLUTION
The Only Way Out

CULTURAL THRESHOLD LEVELS

Every culture has a different social psychology and levels or points at which they just go crazy.

I understand the constant terror of being misjudged. That's one reason I study the holocaust.

I don't care what happened you repent and go on. In an instant you resume your work for the Lord.

For years I reacted violently to uniforms whether policeman or doorman. Ellen Brandt

Everyone wore uniforms because: if you didn't wear one you were non-Aryan, obviously Jewish.

Survivor's kids either wanna know everything about the holocaust or absolutely nothing as it was.

Being marked you got beat up by kids and couldn't object or adults would come and make it worse.

In that milieu what could you expect from your neighbor? Absolutely nothing, never ever.

You couldn't ask and you wouldn't receive a copy of a newspaper even a pencil. You had no radio.

They'd been exposed to the cruelty of the population particularly the children in their uniforms.

It was now seen as patriotic for children to beat up jews and for thug gangs to seek them out too.

SOLITUDE SOLUTION

They gloried in reporting Jews for the slightest infraction or just made stuff up to get a violent reaction.

George Soros was the highest in his life he said, dispossessing the Jews of their livelihoods.

Especially the children were so cruel and self-righteous, having no empathy since that matures last.

Malicious Jezebel was jealous and vindictive so just reported her to the SS and had her arrested.

This reminds me so much of sisters I can't help but think it's a Germanic racial effect on behaviors.

Every culture's different, they all have two sides. Lotsa good points too like they're great scientists.

And now Nazi guilt makes em welcome millions of aliens. See the reversals? It's just fascinatin'

SUSPECT FOR BEING DIFFERENT

You were arrested for anything whatsoever and just for being different you were suspect/it's over.

A sort of patriotic responsibility to beat up on Jews. Unimaginable, does this stun you too?

Not only was it a privilege to abuse/beat up the Jew it made the uniformed children little heroes.

Jews had a peculiar awareness of how the world was crumbling in on them through evil children.

They vilified the peaceful truckers and ignored the violence of burned down cities in summers.

"Slash the tires, empty gas tanks, arrest the drivers and move the trucks" said a CNN analyst.

SOLITUDE SOLUTION

Blanket smear of the dumbed: Everyone becomes a Nazi when you can't argue with them.

CNN and globalist puppets like Trudeau insist on attacking the peaceful protest til they go.

This is a mess, is this a test? But after dust settles I'm left standing there every time, blessed.

He took advantage at a low point with a collapse of boundaries. An empty vessel attracts enemies.

AMBULANCE CHASER

You took advantage of me at a low point. Now I'm up I don't wanna see your face a moral disgrace.

You promised me a motorcade and endless perfume but in one minute you were gone in a feud.

You took advantage when I was down and having lost all morals/boundaries I limply lost my crown.

I don't care what happened when Satan took over the vessel cuz you were a weak embarrassment.

All kinds of crap happens when Satan's the default setting before finding God/heavenly Daddy.

It doesn't matter what it is--you weren't yourself. Another entity had taken over the magic elf.

So forget it now and go on. You haven't much time to do your magical thing for the Lord/the world.

People are creepy and you experienced the worst. But always compare yourself to the holocaust.

That was true hardship--no baths or showers the whole time, one toilet for a thousand people, aye.

SOLITUDE SOLUTION

People complain about trifles/nothing. Just talk to a camp survivor and you'll feel blessed honey.

Forty years the ingrates walked around the mountain to no effect. Stop complaining = success.

DEVIL BRINGS SHAME TO THOUGHTS

It's the devil bringing shame to your thoughts. It's your major block, he knows it, pray you forgot.

If your head as a roof, if you have food, if your spouse isn't rude you're one lucky girl/blessed dude.

It is extremely beneficial both to the world and yourself to learn about the holocaust/grow up fast.

Nationalism isn't Nazism, Donald Trump isn't Hitler. It's good to love your own, patriots are superior.

If you love outsiders more than insiders you're a traitor to your group. That's definitional/true.

Teach disorderly, arrogant, invasive, incorrigible youths of the holocaust to see they're not boss.

In the fifties Americans were grey-suit low-key. They'd seen a catastrophe diminishing the "me".

Teach entitled youth what it's like when everything you own is gone in a minute/ur just a number.

Survivors seem more mature than most. Their priorities are right, they know how life is easily lost.

I learn from survivor stories because I don't see that maturity in the present everyday pansies.

I hate phones, why talk on the phone? He doesn't care if I get headaches he just wants to bloviate.

SOLITUDE SOLUTION

Most had their entire family wiped out, gone forever. A whole generation felt civilization was over.

HOLOCAUST DENIERS ARE COMPLAINERS

That catastrophic milieu was the backdrop creating the social psychology of the fifties: LOW KEY.

It musta been such a shocker when the kids in the sixties became dam hippies even commies.

There was a post-war demon of starvation call anorexia and bulimia exploding all over America.

As a post-war child I had recurrent nightmares of being kidnapped with sounds of dogs and trains.

There's a collective unconscious I was picking up on, being hypersensitive. Nightmares were accurate.

A nightmarish feeling of the collective unconscious was a hole in my gut/bottomless pit/endless rut.

Triple Pisces? I don't know what it was. My brain was always working, I started painting, I was morose.

They detected my differences so I became acquainted with hostility fast and sought privacy [bliss].

ESCPAE INTO SOLITUDE [YOU]

The more privacy I sought the more they invaded me and tried to block my working nonstop.

The only thing that works is finding a husband wanting solitude as much as you. Otherwise stay blue.

Don't be so addicted to your things because they can take it all at 3 a.m. then where would you be.

SOLITUDE SOLUTION

God put holes in the bucket of my thieving opponents but doubled me in houses and view lots.

Finally the tables are starting to turn. Talking about a revolution and the final end of that curse.

People mess up from taking advice of their friends. Pray to God, listen to inner voices which pertain.

They're stuck in blue cities filled with crime/gangs and I'm out here in the beautiful country ok.

It's been so nice talking with y'all. Thank you for being so interested in my worldviews and my fall.

SOCIAL PSYCHOLOGY IS FASCINATING

Because of all I've written I find Social Psychology absolutely fascinating: it's all a herd man.

Like many discoverers have reported in their memoires, it was all inspired by a hit on the head.

It was based on forty years of study and 12 of writing equalling 130 books on social psychology.

I put you in dire circumstances and you adapted like a trooper so now you've a mansion forever.

He's using you as a piece of meat/plumbing. Tell him to GTH cuz to clear eyes it's really sickening.

Instead of self-triggering adrenalin thru memory, think "he was just my lesson in that area."

Leave the past behind, buried in the deepest part of the ocean with a sign "don't go fishing".

The Hero's path ends in success [wholeness] but starts with your Waterloo [battles/a big mess].

SOLITUDE SOLUTION

I had to escape the matrix completely to feel whole again, to be happy and hopeful, to study.

They threw me into comparisons/feeling less than, a painful reduplication of the early system.

THE POTTER'S WHEEL

Being on the Potter's Wheel meant learning how to overcome this social hypnosis of evil.

Learned how evil people can be when they get an edge or talked to someone ruining your rep.

They eclipsed me, walked me by and ridiculed me by comparisons with the peanut gallery.

They're great when you're rich and popular but watch how they hate you as a falling star.

He loved you when you had the penthouse & jaguar but look how he shunned you when poor.

They love you cuz others love you but when they don't you've lost your appeal--it's all SOCIAL.

For it was my best friend who turned his heel against me: that's in Psalms which I read daily.

ONCE IT'S OVER LET IT STAY OVER

Once it's over let it stay over for you now see the thing in reverse: a gestalt-switch has occurred.

It wasn't Borrego, it's all people. But it was an open society so there was no escaping evil.

You see em at the post office, they gossip to those who know you and you sense duplicity too.

SOLITUDE SOLUTION

Stop searching old associations. You're bored or lonely so you fall back but if busy you'd forget em.

It's hard to see the label when you're inside the jar. Try to gain perspective on yourself as star.

People are evil everywhere but in an open society without fences you surely feel it more.

Celebrities are well into parroting the party line of everything from open borders to vaccines.

If you pose a threat to the system now they will simply call you a domestic terrorist to be gone.

For parent terrorists: FBI breaks down door/takes stuff & freezes money, take guns and no-fly list.

I'm done with bullying, blaming, arguing, anger, rudeness, insensitivities, condescension.

The past is my solace. Even WWII era is warmer than this. What has happened to the race?

Even as a five year old I decided I loved men and hated women. It's the truth but hard to admit it.

Had a feminist mother and two liberal sisters. If that's the connection, I have thoughts here.

GOD SHOWS AT LAST MINUTE

You didn't "almost not make it" for God always shows up at last minute so you won't forget it.

My father in heaven showed up & saved me every time at the last minute as if He had planned it.

The purer I got the earlier He'd show up and the less tolerance He had for those abusives.

SOLITUDE SOLUTION

I don't cringe looking back at narrow escapes for I know that's His pattern and there are no delays.

Joined online Calvinist group and felt I entered a meat grinder of left brain scholarly ridicule.

The cross is simple enough for a child or peasant to understand so I've returned to it alone.

The CROSS settles it all. Not one more word need be said. Focus on all He gave you being bled.

Not gonna put up with cum-bay-yah churches neither. I can't stand their silly new hymns either.

Sorry, either it's hellfire sin and repentance, hell and heaven preaching or I'll not be attending.

REPENT YE [THEN GO ON]

The first words of Jesus' in Mathew: "Repent Ye". It's sin holding us back from our destiny.

The CROSS settles it all. Not one more word need be said, it's the new life He gave you being bled.

Bad associations have a way of rubbing off & laying blocks so Jezebels don't get another chance.

Stop remorsing over the past you HAD to endure to learn these precious lessons at last.

People come and they go. It's GOD who is permanent so I'd love Him first THEN those below.

When commie spirit prevails you become frightened of ENVY cuz it leads to violence and calumny.

One way or another Jezebel will aggravate by borrowing things or repeating evil gossip to your face.

SOLITUDE SOLUTION

You're too sweet to take a chance with children of misfortune in this era: have great caution.

With Jezebels it's a dangerous spirit whose only goal is to worm her way in your life and wreck it.

Jezebel is jealous and always will be. It's her middle name, it's in her DNA to be cunning see.

Abused by dad, he came every day and latched on, a sucking spirit taking all not nailed down.

You can't let em in cuz they know no boundaries. They open drawers, closets, anything to see.

THE CHILDREN OF MISFORTUNE

They're the children of misfortune having been taught nothing about decency, boundaries, family.

If parents were drunk kids show the Child of the Alcoholic Syndrome, opposite to a good home.

Children of alcoholics crazy for years don't know it: moral and boundary collapse with trauma.

Child of alcoholic adapts to CYCLES--ups and downs--then projects this misery later in patterns.

Child naturally gravitates to similar characteristics like fawning behavior the next day then a flip.

WHAT MAKES EM IGNORANT?

What makes a narcissist ignorant? Him thinking he knows it all, blocking his enlightenment.

The adult child may have crutches he's used since a kid and he's a mass of devices as an addict.

SOLITUDE SOLUTION

Don't let him in outa pity cuz he'll destroy you. Grifters aren't like dogs or cats who have gratitude.

Don't lend money to these people cuz they won't pay it back and you're just a future target.

With bad endings pay them off just to finish the deal and then future violence is curtailed.

The new foe is frenemies: people you've known or family--the Trump era revealed this anomaly.

Relieve yourself of the BURDEN of inherited guilt and shame which is used to keep you chained.

You may not see it as inherited cuz it feels so personal but it was basic/all thru the family arsenal.

GUILT AND SHAME REPEATS

Go to sleep feeling guilty/wake up feeling shame: the devil's game to keep you spiritually lame.

God doesn't want you feeling guilty, that's not part of His plan. The cross settles it all man.

They're a callous generation cuz they accepted abortion. They're also obese, look at em.

You rose up against me threateningly and that's the same as hitting me it so alarmed me.

Ladies do NOT let a man in your house unless married or chaperoned lest you be overcome/done.

If a man enters your home and takes over he's got murky boundaries, a common problem honey.

When alone in my home it's a starry night but when he enters in it's a madhouse and a fight.

SOLITUDE SOLUTION

STAND UP FOR SOLITUDE/PRIVACY

Stand up for your right to solitude and privacy. It's your constitutional right to be **TRULY FREE.**

There's a prevalent conspiracy against privacy cuz the world wants your attention on it see.

The world tries to guilt trip you for being such a recluse, a hideous stigma especially for the girls.

The world wants you to think you're missing out and uses exclusion as a rudder of control.

I had the most miserable time in a sorority. Somehow I thought it would benefit me socially see.

Stop remorsing over past and just make your mark now. Time is limited and you wanna grow.

A concentration camp victim, a Vietnam vet or an older woman never trusts anyone again.

Especially with the socialist kids you will be attacked for your independent singularity, a private.

It hurts me to be around them they're so rude and callous. A whole generation it seems sis.

But if you will resist everything you hear and forge your way ahead my dear you will **PROSPER.**

As we criminalize parenting we decriminalize criminals and that's the state of our society today.

Controllers have astonishing lack of self-awareness so when you confront get ready for violence.

THE NICE IMAGE OF CONTROLLERS

SOLITUDE SOLUTION

The biggest controller thinks she's the nicest lady you ever met and constantly tells you that.

The biggest controller thinks she's the nicest lady you ever met and constantly tells you that.

See that sweet little lady over there? She's really a scorpion in her dealings so please beware.

Just cuz a sentence isn't executed speedily doesn't mean He's forgotten, just you wait honey.

MOST WOMEN WATCH CNN

Most women know nothing beyond CNN or the opinions of family and friends thus they're dense.

If married to a dumbed down wife and you still go along with her politically you're a cuck of lies.

Just cuz she's so tyrannical always gossipin' to feel legit you wouldn't dare be an bold Trumpist.

Men are conservative in defense of family, home & country but you still listen to your silly lady.

That broad doesn't know a friggin' thing other than CNN & gossipping but you still dig your queen.

He goes along with silly lady--friends & CNN--to have peace cuz if he didn't it means divorce.

Deluded feminist gets her patriot spouse locked up and labeled paranoid psychotic when pissed.

Deluded brainwashed feminist gets estranged husband's gun taken, that'll surely fix him.

He needs those guns to protect you witch but you're so ignorant you just tear down your house.

SOLITUDE SOLUTION

Nothing divides families like Christ or Trump. Enraged wives all over America husband-dumped.

In Protestantism it's the cross plus *nothing* but in false churchism is a buncha other things.

THE WHOLE WORLD IS EVIL

Instead of anger at people see entire world as evil so without boundaries the problem was you.

You're angry at certain people but the world is full of evil so see the macro and build a fence too.

The false church adds endless new requirements for salvation when there's only one, amen.

Instead of anger at individual soldiers the survivor sees war itself as catastrophe and torture.

It was WAR for an introverted single female without a fence or verbal skill sets in her defense.

I had no idea I could just say "I don't want a man in my house alone" or "I WANT TO BE ALONE."

The grifter said I was rude for not letting him in my house and I was so dense I let in the louse.

Give me sin/repentance hell/heaven preaching or tell deacons it's a false church happening.

The modern church avoids sin and hell sermons because all donations would stop in a minute.

Everything you went through you had to go through to learn that lesson through and through.

The modern church avoids sin and hell sermons cuz all donations would stop or worsen.

SOLITUDE SOLUTION

This is the greatest country in the world. You can start with nothing and become everything girl.

MEMORY IS THE DEVIL'S TOOL

The devil's greatest tool to keep you down is MEMORY of the foolish things you did, a clown.

Just when feeling good about yourself Satan pops a morbid/embarrassing memory like a pill.

Seeing bad memories as the devil's device powers you to substitute them with new things in life.

Each dawn is a new beginning despite yesterday's sinning and seeing it this was is godly.

No matter WHAT you did, start again and keep starting again. Don't let bad patterns reset in.

Yes it's horrible what he did to you but life's a bitch until you learn those special lessons–did you?

Land of Milk and Honey: butter, cheese, cream brings strength and satiety not just fruit & veggies.

I live in fear of the Spirit of Familiarity so I think spouses should separate regularly even all day.

I'm never bored nor lonely so I need NO one for entertainment or for supposed flattery.

"You look so good for your age" brings reactions of "F-U for your backhanded complements".

AGEIST COMMENTS

One way or the other they gotta get it in there: ageist comments making them feel superior.

SOLITUDE SOLUTION

Despite the media protection racket Joe Biden's ratings are plummeting faster than a rocket.

When are you married? When he goes into her tent, that's the Old Testament way of doing it.

Jezebel always causes division. You were mean to me cuz she primed you ever so innocently.

If you're always yelling at past enemies in your head--what you shoulda said--clarity is dead.

There's no way you can get outa the survival need for forgiveness, if not for pure selfishness.

GOOD IS BAD AND BAD IS GOOD

In this generation good is called bad, and bad good. Sweet is really bitter, and bitter sweet--understood?

Just why do you put up with these people, I ask? The desire to be seen as social is such a painful task.

Dis-attend from most of what you see, it's a ripoff. Meanwhile don't trust many friends, they give tip-offs.

It's a bad thing to be taken through your needs for flattery. Learn to see all impostors as in a gallery.

HOOKED TO REJECTION CHEMICALS

Since the narc produces the most chemicals we're hooked on, in the trauma we rehook to him: no fun.

The narcissist produces a contagion of lunacy as it's not just you but anyone you talk to, see?

With you going no-contact the narc gets new supply immediately--it's astonishing but don't dismay.

SOLITUDE SOLUTION

The ART of going no-contact must be practiced and practiced more--for empaths it's really hard.

The victim gets re-ensnared out of pity and the narcissist knows just what to say to his old lady.

Make no-contact be the order of the day/entire focus since success comes from the space created.

Having cleared out all non-essential superfluity what is left is our beautiful home estate, so pretty!

EMOTIONAL DEPLETION

Every time you go there/yield to him you are defeated--frustrated, hurt, angry: YOU DON'T NEED IT.

You will never hurt me again. Do your own thing but don't come to me cuz I'm IMMUNE/not your friend.

There's a reason I'm like this now: you hurt me. This reason I put ever before me to stop sympathy.

It's a serious situation--you triggering early trauma--but in the long run it's better: must face it to love again.

The more pain you cause [chemicals aroused] the more I want YOU [to heal those early attachments lost].

Thus it's crucial to milk this juncture in your journey--you've reached a fork in the road, believe me.

He gets worse so the more you procrastinate to eliminate the more you'll be wiped out in great probability.

As he gets worse to get back at you [for whatever] he brings himself down: just wait/don't get involved.

He makes stupid mistakes [on the wrong premise it's based] and makes an ass of himself: just wait.

SOLITUDE SOLUTION

You will NOT reel me back in, you will NOT blow hot and cold cuz I won't know about it, that's all.

STOP NEEDING THE OUTER WORLD

Stop needing messages from the outer world. Stop looking and lurking: only God should be preferred.

The way they eat is pure lawlessness. The outcome in looks and health is disastrous, so be cautious.

Love your husband or wife no matter what you feel about them. It's a choice not a feeling, amen?

I'm ready to rule. I've been through graduate school: bullied like a fool I found the true by being un-cool.

The victim constructs high walls against the whole world, as a wretched personality disorder unfurls.

Soon the victim hates everyone good or bad. He lashes out indiscriminately, seen as a wicked cad.

TV: As brainwaves and IQ's lower we go into a highly suggestible trancelike state--too dumb to be irate.

The victim begins to lose all boundaries. Desperate for love, the bad streams in (more subtle bullies).

The movies are all about revenge. This scratches an itch for the fringe: women having an edge.

Eagle-eyed and poker-faced: That's the look of tyranny as freedoms are erased and life debased.

Even in a rotten climate we can still make it. Just look UP (not down) then repent so God can bring it.

It's all about defending their sins which they love. You don't? You're out. Forgive, then be a dove.

SOLITUDE SOLUTION

Never apologize for power. It was hard work and grit making us the man/woman/country of the hour.

Is your style gangsta or your unique identity? That's once in a time, never before seen through eternity.

OBSESSIONS FROM EARLY TRAUMAS

He produces the chemicals your entire being is hooked on and this means you're obsessed hon'.

Don't start the "what if" crap. Just by ghosting or disappearing he's disrespecting, face that.

Get to know the narcissist lingo [a complete science now] to notice instantly when he blows hot and cold.

You feel like a heroin addict unless you break away, STAY AWAY and heal from this peptide addiction.

Be strong--be true to yourself, hon'. It never gets better only worse but can be used to fix what stung.

The only answer is to self-partner, meet our trauma and release it. So mom never liked you, forget it.

Stalking the creep on social media is as bad as doing drive-bys or asking their friends for more lies.

Stalk him on social media: peptide addiction increases. Stop it immediately: soon wellness/happiness.

If still suffering traumas in the body due to abandonment at this point she may surge after the narcissist.

Your answer is to soothe the young unhealed terror of not being loved/rejected in your early years on earth.

Narcs don't wanna lose their supply so they make contact on random things to test the waters by and by.

SOLITUDE SOLUTION

They're like crocodiles keeping lumps of meat under a rock for chew later on. Don't allow it: be done.

He asks cryptic questions or makes suggestions that are confusing all to get your head spinning.

HIS COLDNESS TRIGGERS TERROR

His coldness triggers the terror of early childhood and makes her love him more, seen as "good".

It's too easy and self-defeating to stalk someone on social media so stop it now or there's no real healing.

Stop putting down women and their cats. They're all we have and you're causing cat abuse you cad.

Keep em on their toes by keeping em confused: "there's someone at my door" [is he seeing someone else?]

He wants to see if you'll be triggered/what you're gonna do so he can reel you back in: don't be a fool.

If you break no-contact and resume engaging you'll again fall unconscious into questions/begging.

Accept that any more stalking/engaging will be ONLY traumatic, confusing, invalidating and painful.

Healing remedy is: don't engage, maintain no-contact, purge thoughts of him: this is DETOX.

If you go back the narc will get you worse cuz he's miffed you made him vulnerable/have to kiss up.

Once their ego defenses come flying back up again they are worse than before, count on it forever.

The narc does terrible things to trigger and get your attention and it's horrible when it happens.

SOLITUDE SOLUTION

It includes abuse by proxy, smearing/discrediting or stealing, damaging property, hurting loved ones.

He will try to destroy your life in any way he can: you made him feel vulnerable by your objections.

EXPECT HIS/HER PUNISHMENTS

He's punishing for not appeasing his false self and a warped belief of what you did to him—a projection.

This two-pronged attack is a way to get your attention and to hand over narcissistic supply now man.

If you were one who fought back while in relationship you were even more A-grade supply for his kingship.

We then become the dumpster they can offload their wounds onto and INTO. Release or be blue!

If he/she knows you fight back, you're a target for these down-putting tactics. Set a boundary, they attack.

To heal, STOP that part of you seeking to heal, help or change crazily abusive people: do this NOW.

When you pull away, detach and heal all that comes up and is triggered within you a new life's in view.

Know you are an honest, decent person walking that straight line and the truth will do the rest.

Heal all triggers coming up within you and you'll discover all his sly antics fall on deaf ears: whew!

To ever go back to his [house, channel, space] is pure masochism, an accident waiting to happen.

For he can say/display anything, start smearing/confusing, describe a new fling: make it NOT happening.

SOLITUDE SOLUTION

He only wants to superiorize over you. He's an adolescent in his short fuse: lock your gate or be blue!

ONLY ONE, THE REST SHUN

Let him know there's only **ONE** who superiorizes over you: your own husband and that's not him, amen.

Marry a deeply devoted man then stay within those walls--no more communicating outside with rabble.

DETOX is dispersing all the crap they put in you. Since that's the goal, help it along--walk, rest, song.

You must **SEE** that internet stalking is **AS BAD** as parking in front of his house. Get some class, lass.

You're putting him first instead of yourself--always seeking **OUTER** validation by some louse!

With unhealed wounds from early trauma, the new guy rejecting us makes us think he's **MOMMA**.

In response to his abuse the best course of action is to be **AUTHENTIC**. Move on and don't try to get back.

The narc will always move on and immediately replace you with new supply. **EXPECT** this/refuse to cry.

RELATE to your new positive youtube mentors. Let them pour in a new reality: strong, relentless, fearless.

DIVIDE evil from good. The narcissist is evil who hurts you, your youtube mentors are good helping you.

Hold onto them for awhile. Make playlists of their best, hear them all day long while recalling his guile.

SOLITUDE is your highest therapy. That means not just physical aloneness but social media avoidance.

SOLITUDE SOLUTION

It used to be you could erase an ex quick. But now with the ease of internet stalking we just stay sick.

BE A SELF-PARTNER

Be a self-partner: be an adult not letting your [inner] child go out to play with someone you deemed bad, ok?

Once you've grieved the original wound this guy won't have ANY influence--it's just that simple girl.

Whether he's a young beta loser or a dirty old man, either way finish the transition and you're all-ok.

To the narc you're an object performing a role. There's no one home to love you, give up that goal.

When he sees your ship going down there's another one waiting at the dock: supply comes first/well stocked.

Replacement is extreme trauma like your ancient DNA: starving to death or being thrown outa the hut.

Return to your home of true loving support and wall out the rest: the land of deception for sport.

The triggering of ancient DNA shows how EXTREME replacement can feel, I remember it well.

It can trigger such panic and without the adult tools to deal with it even one's self-worth feels illigit.

The answer is SOLITUDE to forget this Jezebel/dude. It's not about them but original trauma in childhood.

I believe REPLACEMENT is the most horrible thing we can go through, bringing mal-adaptive coping devices.

The reactive female may fight back with bad choices, sexual affairs, addictions, falling into depression.

SOLITUDE SOLUTION

REACTION IN SEXUAL AFFAIRS

The reactive female fighting back through sexual affairs makes things so much worse for herself I declare.

I'm giving you the tools to fight this without resorting to self-destructive devices--just learn the patterns.

The healing remedy is this: HEAL IT. Go inside as if it's a raw wound in self-partnering: you deserve it.

Visualize your inner child, abandoned. Load it up, cry then release it--bringing in your True Self replacement.

Finally, you'll be rid of all the ENVY/pain connected to any narcissistic relationship, all of it gone forever.

Once healed let nature take it's course. His new supply is on the same journey ending in the worst.

Once healed you evolve to a Higher Relationship Imprint in your future, FAR higher than when immature.

RISE ABOVE AS THE NEW BRASS

When all have lost their moral compass and acting like an ass, repent and rise up as the new brass.

Make good use of your time by improving your mind. That's NOT Fox News (becoming a grind).

Medium Chill: Cordial without letting them abuse you. That's how you treat liberals in the family or pew.

The very people assigned to protect us have been wimped by their angry wives. A sad situation, no jive.

Just because they're zombies doesn't make em harmless. Get involved with any one = no more calmness.

Though a "master", does he have wide-angled vision? Does he see the whole,

SOLITUDE SOLUTION

does he have a mission?

When faced with toxic fury then sheepish conciliatory apologies: let them go, that's all you need to know.

Over-concern for looks marked Rome before it's fall: vanity everywhere yet none walked tall.

When we transcend chaos it always feels the same: extreme exhilaration as eternity is reclaimed.

If women are good to men the results increase a hundredfold. To a good man, a sweet female is gold.

We're supposed to go along with anything trendy though it means getting smutty and putting down daddy.

There is not one but two separate realities: Male and female--when the latter dominates, big penalties.

They want us messed up by weak men and angry women. That's been the plan all along by evil vermin.

UTTER CRUELTY IS ALL OK-ED

The utter cruelty in society is being downplayed. Everyone senses it but no one says it: it's all O.K.'d.

Some women are mad because they think they're supposed to be. When free of fake roles, they're free.

What is the best teacher? Having your faced pushed in the mud--a Ph.D. in the streets by Elmer Fudd.

Men are always apologizing for supposed anti-female slights. This is so sad too--it's just not right.

Stop being victims of pop culture wanting you degraded so the richest nation is brought low, glory faded.

SOLITUDE SOLUTION

38,000 suicides a year and 30,000 of them are men. The female victims have become the abusers, amen.

They're trying to remove all boundaries, leaving us in a cesspit of collectivism and immorality.

The ultimate goal of the toxic abuser is making you question your sanity. They rule reality, though it's inanity.

Stupid women tear their house down. In angry tears they drown when they coulda worn a crown.

If a woman is cruel and a man so wimped he can't be trusted, what is the child but self-disgusted?

TOUGH LOVE IS JUST BEING MEAN

They call it "tough love" but it's just being mean. Even the strong are intimidated by trendies: society's fiends.

I thought it was just me invaded by insanity until I asked and found you all have tolerated profanity.

Just because one's rich doesn't make em good, sane or humane. But these elites rule in the main.

They don't want equality but privileges with NO responsibility. You must see this with your best ability.

People are about image not reality: they are image-magicians. For these types, stop fishin'.

Turn it all off and avoid those who scoff nonstop as you review all you've learned and now, the payoff.

God made all this and if they can't see it they have a stony heart. God made us too--soon we'll do our part.

The ego-driven narcissist sees only his own world, not the true external. Dense until death, the eternal.

SOLITUDE SOLUTION

When sin hardens the heart they get snippy, weird, mean: They become insensitive, losing their sheen.

If you take back a cheater it'll be worse next time, for in this generation they failed to draw that line.

Judge Judy is obviously anti-male. Women are gaining control, setting up sadly used men to fail.

Instead of letting em in and saying you're gonna be big why not be big and never let em in (and don't renege).

When chaos reaches critical mass you sense it's all gas. This marks your time has come: the new brass.

Nowadays the girl's are audacious and the boys timid. These are the trends, increasingly wicked.

FEMINISM IS SPLITTING FAMILIES

Once she turns kids against father now she turns them against sister, boyfriend, aunt--whatever.

Transcend levity. That's meaningless jocularity, not being a rarity. Life is serious so don't be petty.

Women aren't supposed to act that way (inferior). They were right and perfect before (superior).

We all know a good female role model. Just emulate her not the modern day rabble (they are awful).

When the fake talk they use too many words. All the wrong angles, the irrelevant or mostly just slurs.

Men, stop apologizing. It's pathetic you've been pushed this far but just repent and be uncompromising.

MOST EVIL IS SOCIAL HYPNOTISM

SOLITUDE SOLUTION

Most evil is social hypnotism: tolerating increased levels of perverse badness--that's new wave feminism.

Two causes of bullies: a tortured soul just wanting love or revenge/rage they can't let go of.

As people side against the victim he becomes an untouchable. How sad--aren't humans despicable?

The bullied begins to feel there is no hope. He loses all boundaries so as the sharks move in he can't cope.

Sometimes we stay when we should leave and visa-versa. Being where you don't belong causes inertia.

You never know one till you see him in all situations. Then you can trust with out surprise/degradation.

They don't care about human rights they only care how they're dressed: heartless and superficial pests!

STAY HIGHNESS NO MATTER WHAT

See yourself as the King (no cuss). You must lest you rust in self-disgust, mal-adapting to the lush.

What you see on TV is awful. Debauchery, licentiousness, betrayal and anything else unlawful.

Never think popularity shows truth or rightness. More often it's bunk--the herd is consensual blindness.

Never judge value by how popular it is. The best thing the herd can't see--that's how good it is.

They fake "loving" to serve their gushing identity. It's not who they are at all, there's no real serenity.

We'll never be equal and thus communism implies tyranny: You gotta lop off heads to equalize you and me.

SOLITUDE SOLUTION

INFLUENCE FEMININE OR FEMINIST?

Feminine or feminist influence? Two separate things: one sings, the other destroys the home/has flings.

If you're great, expect hate. Envy is the reason for bullying so harden up but be kind (not irate).

People befriend victim just to use him some more. They get what they want then push him out the door.

They'll stop at nothing to buttress their fake ideas. It's all a surface party line cruel as North Korea's.

Having an inferior over you arouses jealousy of his power. Don't refuse to obey, soon it's your hour.

They say men die early due to their jobs--not. It's due to feminist insults, flings and divorce--rot.

Most niceness is fake--they just want approval for the ego's sake. A plastic world is a constant dull ache!

Watch out for the guy who says he's for the poor but only hangs with the rich--he's married to a witch.

FEMALE ACCUSATIONS AND ADDICTIONS

Mad women report men for everything (false allegations). Guns, rape, abuse and other vindictive accusations.

A sick generation justifies it's addictions and calls it science. Of false teachers make **NO** allowance.

They're so evil this will be a turkey-shoot. The harvest is ripe for true evangelicals in their champion suit.

The kids couldn't be any more lewd. They're even proud of it so there's no debating they're crude, dude.

SOLITUDE SOLUTION

We live in a cesspool. Criminal politicians, perverts common, everybody robbin', outa their noggin.

What's it take to wake you up--you brainwashed children of the left? Nothing--with trifles you're obsessed.

It's all a flock/herd flying in perfect unison with each other--the opposite of the higher brain, but whatever...

Humans have always been the same. They form in cliques then everyone else is seen as lame.

They actually think they're loving. It's all just ideology but takes over the mind anyway, say goodbye okay?

They want "diversity of views" as long as we agree with theirs. They're a terrible threat--our peers.

DUMMY GENERATION BY DESIGN

CNN is a globalist machine--thugs, fiends.

If your church has morphed you become a spiritual dwarf. The false church is boring, and forced.

Pervasive homosexuality in Hitler's top levels: The Pink Swastika.

Earth shattering insight and bad effects: men have half the testosterone of fifty years back.

You'd have to be totally dumbed down, blind and hypnotized to vote for him/her--but that's you, sir.

A dummy generation by design. It's more serious than you can know: gross not refined.

Pear--shaped men with scruffy beards/man boobs. Since soy's in everything, they look silly: lopsided, bloated, flaky too.

In the land of zombies you into truth are rejected by family and friends. Hope this helps you to mend.

SOLITUDE SOLUTION

Give up on them, they know nothing. These are your liberal friends who justify/condone everything.

The human group is marked by envy, jealousy, misfits and scapegoats. Reject these cut-throats.

Watch out for duplicitous witches--the ones from high school you thought were your friends. Now, mend.

Spring Break shows why we're going down: Total moral decay and apathy as troops invade our towns.

Women think they get ahead by pushing men down. From this comes terrible tragedies all around.

Groups think alike. They monitor behavior to prevent differences or a spike much like the Third Reich.

Disliking anyone who makes them think, they hate the messenger who's not like them—how rinky-dink.

PEOPLE ARE TRIBAL: UNTRUE

People are tribal, thinking truth is defined by the group--the opposite is true, that's the scoop.

These kids are totally unprepared for what's about to happen while they're nappin and so spoiled rotten.

They started as hippies from the sixties. Now they're leftist professors bringing us down swiftly.

They're primed in childhood so how could they think any different? They're dumbed down, not brilliant.

He puts down Christians and Jews but never them (his people). He sees us in the pews as pure evil.

Evil minimizes evil because it's conscience is seared with a hot iron. Stand strong against this, hon'.

SOLITUDE SOLUTION

Stop apologizing for being male. This is all from the feminist takeover and you're being set up to fail.

True reality is seen by clear people. But evil can't see evil and thus "everything is equal".

The abortion culture is so desensitized it has no empathy. No more do we defend the weak, incredibly.

We're all looking for an escape. Those who don't see a reason to are more than I can take--what fakes.

When the wicked rule the people mourn. Fear, anger, depression--some wish they were never born.

The phony hypocrisy of some women: They're all for "liberation" but when one raises up, they'll kill em.

STEERING PUBLIC OPINION WITH ILLOGIC

These broads steer public opinion with illogic (being minions) changing hearts and minds of millions.

The left smiles for awhile: They give you things, have flings, say silly things but beneath it's all guile.

Tyrants always replaced God with the state to take rights. Feminists led the way in this fight.

Men please stop saying you're sorry. It's really pathetic you buying this line from ladies gone awry.

Collectivism only exists through the group mentality: pitting one group against another (dad by the mother).

It's sin, my friend. Don't listen to liberals and trends--in crossing that line you've become blind again.

The dense minimize--they don't see a threat--but a nightmare of epic proportions is seen by the vets.

SOLITUDE SOLUTION

A college degree means nothing if it's all about revised history, stupid. It's all politics not learning, deluded.

SAINTS ARE MILD AND SOBER

The saints are mild and sober. They aren't garrulously smiley/know life's tragedies as mindful voters.

Constant chaos and jocularity is such a bore! This is the adulterous generation I've learned to abhor.

Feminism's taken over, not about women but destroying family and dividing us more than ever.

The gangsta nation encourages false identities just to not be killed by surrounding enemies.

True power has finesse, compassion and mercy. That's missing in a woman's wrath when bloodthirsty.

You've had to tolerate liberal logic for decades, never knowing that was the problem--but it was Hades.

They say they're "happy" but in truth they're viscous pill-poppers, all from their doctor's orders.

AT SOME POINT YOU LET IT ALL GO

At some point you give up all carnal or worldly interests. The news doesn't amuse and it's ignorance.

Just when things look indomitable, invincible, impossible--it can still be done cuz fighting giants is fun.

Laughter's like cackling thorns on the fire. It's so irritating, wish they'd just shut up, these thieves and liars.

The modern church has lost it's fire. In becoming milquetoast the dumbed have lost all will to aspire.

SOLITUDE SOLUTION

In 1962 they took God outa the schools and the result is a nation of poor fools who think they're cool.

Depravity and dumbness go together. As a nation degrades, so too looks (skin like leather).

It all started in the sixties by the hippies: relaxed sexual standards and the results weren't pretty.

What blocks this great capacity for man's visions? it is outer entertainment--less is more fishin'.

Women actually think anti-depressants are "happy pills". They're being killed from slums to Beverly Hills.

So you gotta "Like" from a dummy. That shouldn't be your end goal honey and it makes no money.

Once they cross that line they justify it all no matter how bad--let alone being unkind or unrefined.

THE TOLERANT ARE MOST INTOLERANT

These are the people you gotta watch out for. So-called "tolerants" are really intolerant to the core.

Cops: If they don't get in trouble for laying it on double it'll happen more as all our rights crumble.

On facebook, interacting with scum will make you a bum. You settle for less and it makes you a mess.

Are you guys drunk on occult symbolism? The half-times are disgusting as we go into communism.

Born this way: its a logical progression to include pedophilia in this crap--what a day.

They say pedophilia's okay if you're "born that way". How low societies go when evil elite have their way.

SOLITUDE SOLUTION

Haha: Grown adults desperate for "likes" while their own situation can take a hike--yikes!

It's an emergency situation and no one seems to care ("whatever") only caring for their own pleasure.

MOST PEOPLE DON'T STUDY

Many people don't study they just repeat what they've heard. A dangerous thing if you listen to the herd.

They'll be arrogant to the end, then a giant crash when they see they have no friends. Sin = descend.

We've reached a level of utter depravity. Even the music industry is furthering their cause callously.

When their personal reality is the whole thing there's little you can do. To tell the truth, that was me too.

Since most all are sick, we gotta think how to transcend all this and stay quick. Solution: pick.

What flipped the switch turning the sweet lady into a witch? Her feminist friends scratch an itch.

MEN: PLEASE STOP APOLOGIZING

Men: Stop apologizing--it's gone far enough. This is all a leftist conspiracy to make you un-tough.

You know that's not true, why encourage her view? She's ruined your sons and daughters too.

Shame on you, instilling this crap. It's false, dirty and nasty--you should just evoke their own map.

Oh what the heck we're going into robotism anyway. First us then liberals if they have their way.

SOLITUDE SOLUTION

Judge Judy is mean to men. She interrupts, ridicules and punishes for non-issues, no friend.

They laugh, they smile but inside they're filled with guile. Meanwhile it all goes to hell for 4000 miles.

It's the fact that he minimizes this torture that we hate his guts--no conscience or just nuts?

After Ms. Obama pulled the salt and fat from school lunches, now the children have no joy or hunches.

Evil can't see evil so it goes blindly on and it's truly despicable as they wear a smiley and seem amiable.

What sets off the different sides? Toxins, alcohol/drugs, media and people are the great divides.

Just becuz you're artistic, neat and love antiques doesn't make you gay. Many great normies were that way.

Women get furious because they think they're supposed to be: they've been primed by the TV.

She controls through malicious gossip and slander. A viscous enemy, we tippy-toe to avoid her anger.

They feel dapper as they run off to war, but soon (both them and the girls) will see many things to abhor.

Both sexes have become narcissistic, furthered by their internet selections of self, sin, even the sadistic.

EVERYTHING REFLECTS *HER*

Everything she sees is a reflection of her. It must: If it isn't she disses it and becomes the admonisher.

What is a witch? A rejected female who wants to get back at men through potions, hexes or comedienne.

SOLITUDE SOLUTION

Woman admire Judge Judy as a model of how they should act. Put-downs and prejudice, not the facts.

A "folie a deux" is a gruesome twosome--a dysfunctional relationship of two. Could this be you?

The world has gone completely mad and little ladies have become pugnacious--dangerous bad fad.

The condemned hang together like peas in a pod. Meanwhile the chosen are alone, supported by God.

Amongst a mass of liberalism, a few champs stand out. Their job is to stay on top despite envy, no doubt.

Why should they have control over our health decisions or whether we smoke pot? It's a net, we're caught.

You voted for them and now we're all going into servitude: debt and taxes by a bunch of lying asses.

It's truly disgusting as selfishness sets in. From a family matriarch to a shark--and can be no friend.

The preacher said it was all-okay, he even married em to be part of the fray cuz they called it gay.

Low expectations is soft bigotry. Aspire--never tire--and you'll rise up while coming through brilliantly.

Obamanoids: the dumbest people on earth but that doesn't make them less treacherous---need rebirth.

YOU'RE TOO SENSITIVE FOR THIS WORLD

Some people are just too sensitive for this world. In that event, be kind but detached, especially if a girl.

In times of great transition, now's the time to hold to the rigid line: Don't listen and stay refined.

SOLITUDE SOLUTION

You get to a point where you can't tell yourself stories anymore. Denial hurts--close that old door.

They could never stand being told what to do. It's a nation of sloth and sluggards (more than a few).

God: when will you turn on my persecutors? They're heady, they're wrong, they're the throng, the worst.

Aging baby boomers, unite! Learn the facts and then mature beyond our liberals leader (our blight).

Marriage: don't delay it and stay in it. What we have now is serial mourning of lost affections and rejection.

Everything they say is backwards and the victims are you, bro' and sis! They aren't lovers but fascists.

You know what? FOX sux. The clear are sick of the left's interruptions: only truth rocks.

Now is the time for all real men to come forward! What we have now is apathy to this horror.

The bible stories are about overcoming impossible situations and "invincible" enemies: let it be.

Another regulation to "protect" us from ourselves. One thing I know: they are the hawks, we the doves.

If he's successful the bully just gets more brazen. Fight back or he becomes a worse poison.

When we lose the internet you won't be able to express yourself again or hear the truth of friends.

FAKE PREACHERS ARE MILQUETOAST

Due to fake preachers people are destroyed from lack of knowledge and it won't help going to college.

SOLITUDE SOLUTION

Feminist slogans are getting increasingly ridiculous. Take it from me, these broads are duplicitous.

If you must copy someone, let it be from a saner generation. One with class not acting like an ass.

Without quality there can be no equality. Unless feigning and faking is your major policy (wantonly).

In dysfunctional marriages the buddies are more important than the bride and alcohol makes them snide.

The problem is they get so much confirmation for the gangster type, the gentler men can take a hike.

Feminists say men are horrible and mean. They must be resisted somehow, that's the whole scene.

As men lost the support of women, only an adversarial relationship remained. Men are worse off unchained.

Left to themselves they just get more bullish. Women have a refining influence--not so childish.

The degraded male image combines with bad father templates and the result: you're seen as bad mates.

Fed by feminist slogans the wife gets self-involved and tries out roles while nothing is solved.

GANG MENTALITY TRIFLES IN CYCLES

It's all a gang mentality now--a matter of survival. It becomes evil, warring over trifles in cycles.

Tell your child: stay away from strangers. That's everyone in the schools, even teachers fraught with dangers.

It is gross and unrefined. What ever happened to the gentile sophistication of past eras, friends of mine?

SOLITUDE SOLUTION

So much narcissism in the gym. That's the new "in" but without a renewed mind things stay grim

She may hate it when his buddy has influence over him--but did he feel abandoned by the mannish woman?

Because of this grosser male temperament, women have a lot more to deal with each moment.

It takes very little to tick them off. That's the new manliness but it's fake and dangerous--no payoff.

Don't feel bad if you don't fit the new system of fakes, drags and cads. It's all very sad how they get mad.

The wicked struts and the vilest of men are promoted. It's all due to the filthy fakes for whom you voted.

Cheap preachers give them a license to sin. God's gonna get you all--consigned to the hell trash bin.

Ideas are bullet-proof: I will transcend my detractors cuz I was designed to do this, in God's favor.

The characteristic of liberals is blurred lines. Watch out for your husband/wife--keep em in line.

I'm done. For eight years it was no fun as each day a new shoe would drop and now they want the guns.

PULL THE PLUG ON MIND-CLUTTER

Pull the plug on mind-clutter. That's the dense hierarchies, peddled fictions and things from the gutter.

Old ugly harridans are heading all departments. It's a nightmarish tyranny calling for anti-depressants.

The bible says to avoid worthless, futile debate. They're utopians not realists and just get irate.

SOLITUDE SOLUTION

Finding God is just like coming home. I tried being "loving" but it was fake, my star left un-shone.

The bible says not to fear. It's hard when you see all the contradictions and takeovers, as a seer.

The biggest side-effect of anti-depressants is: depression. Think on this then start to question.

What's a superior man? It's about character and restraint: drawing lines so you're ready when it hits the fan.

It's basically the youth but the old ones too: They adapt to buddies, unprepared when all hell ensues.

Due to drugs the kids are asleep. It's such a shame as childhood is dulled and they become creeps.

Old age is characterized by lucid recall. As the body recedes we see eternity and have a ball.

Don't be fooled by things sounding good but lifeless as wood. Only liberty--like in childhood.

70% of pharma-pill poppers are not sick! They've been pushed into it by slick doctors--tricked.

I'd rather be in the wilderness than all those lies. Everyday interactions: demons in disguise.

The trendy generation are in for a big surprise. They think they're "hip" but it's all about to flip.

HELL: LIVING WITH FEMINIST SLOGANS

Living with feminist slogans is a kind of hell. The sweet lady is silent, not constantly ringing ego's bell.

In Al-Anon, wives of alcoholics gossip about their husbands. That's how they fight, it's like a clubbin'.

SOLITUDE SOLUTION

Sex role reversals don't work. There's a natural division of labor but the natural is out of favor.

Oprah is a false prophet of nothingness. Her religion won't help you--only Jesus not wisdom of shrews.

It's other people who bring us down while smiling all around. it's la-la land, ideology and dumbed down.

Can a woman drive a man to drink? Yes, if she's a feminist it's an endless argument--it's how they think.

Few politicians are statesmen. The latter care about their country, the others are just businessmen.

Whether you're creative or not depends a lot on the lies you bought or obstruction (mental clot).

We're so needy we live for likes. This is so juvenile and pathetic for a man or woman of God--Yikes!

How easily we divide when media is our guide! They want us fighting with each other, not allied.

Who are they really, behind the mask? Finding this out is an easy task: just wait, no need to ask.

Told to be strong, women copy men. That isn't it--it's the female attributes and being a true friend.

COLOR IS JUST A DIVISIVE TACTIC

They say it's all about color. This is just a divisive tactic to hide what they're doing while undercover.

Children are fine until adolescence then dark themes threaten their essence despite your patience.

Don't get too much into news, TV etcetera. We all know it's the scariest it's ever been for America.

SOLITUDE SOLUTION

We all want to be accepted. But unfortunately that's a lousy reason to get elected--it's very deceptive.

Where are the true ladies? They're being driven crazy, daily--by silly sayings making life weighty.

With time the most horrible things go mainstream. We desensitize until things aren't what they seem.

The liberal public schools had different effects. Some go to crime, some to grime and others to illicit sex.

Trump outlawing cliteroectomies/arresting the doctors doing em. Liberals all for this barbarity, the dung!

Trump is mentally ill because he believes men should be strong?

The political use of psychiatry by authoritarian regimes is certain and now we see it again it seems.

Anyone who wants to be somebody is a "narcissist" and they've added hundred new diseases to assist.

The feminist says her sister has "delusions of grandeur" cuz she dreams of future greatness: a sickness!

"President Donald Trump is a hostile revisionist power dedicated to overturn the U.S.-led liberal order."

Thinking you're successful is insane to those who want to control or make you go away.

LIBERALS HATE OUR CONFIDENCE

Since when is confidence a mental illness: "narcissist"?

Before I was rich he treated me despicably. But then he started to kissup like a crybaby and so predictably.

Liberals don't care about women, animals, home or country cuz they love Islam--notice how contradictory.

SOLITUDE SOLUTION

The snooty feminist raised four fools. They thought they were cool but fell when used as the devil's tools.

He was so cruel and dismissive, the awful things he said! I blocked all who like him, they're dead.

In case you haven't noticed, FOX has gone left suddenly. This change of guard is liberal and ugly.

Dems know it's about getting votes from the most (the common man) but then later, we're toast.

Trump is truth and that's why the sudden revitalization movement into another poli-psychology.

We must attack the politically correct as the setup for Hitler. Speak: don't be quiet, dry or bitter.

We worship the scum who are our oppressors? The ones who say we're bad as the aggressors?

How we feel with the Trump guy: "Where the spirit of the Lord is, there is liberty" 2 Cor. 3:17

What is "Americana"? Privacy: We hate snitches, but that's how sinners get, scum or witches.

OBVIOUS: DEMOCRATS HAVE NO MORALS

The filthy democrats have no morals. Evil things they condone (common core) they take as gospel.

Rich filth: The evil have become affluent. The bible says not to fear, soon they will be absent.

These people are sickening! Yet they've been in power over us? Lord, please give us a quickening!

We got a dirty rotten traitor and they got back five major killers and our rulers are our pillars?

SOLITUDE SOLUTION

Our ruin came from white communists with tenure. We must control these college professors.

Most liberals are nice people--they just wanna get along--but voting in evil is where they go wrong.

Expose Hillary for the leftist harridan she is. Bernie was put in to make her look centrist, though a trash bin.

Used to see greatness in rulers but now just drama: Selfies and fame while creating ruin and trauma.

It is frightening to see how far Democrats has fallen. And your friends go along with these Stalins.

They took away Washington/Lincoln and replaced with MLK Jr. It's commies replacing us/ruining our future.

Have they built anything--products and services we need? No, they're politicians keeping us unfree.

Privacy is an inalienable right and God hates snitches. This is Americana: nonconformity is the riches.

RETURNING FROM THE BRINK

God could change His mind in punishing us. We've gone so wrong but things could change for us.

WOW! Whatever he says comes true. First they hate him then see he's right--- Donald's so cool.

This is the Man of the Hour, the only one giving us hope. He rings true, every word, and they are dopes.

Trump is our only hope, otherwise we look back at this evil empire where good is bad and bad has power.

How long will the moderate left stay silent on Antifa? The mayors, politicians, deans: it's obscene.

SOLITUDE SOLUTION

Cowards like Pelosi are just using Antifa to their benefit to cow free speech against them.

You must confront your politicians and say "do you support Antifa and their violence?" (sadistic).

Antifa is a political militia doing the bidding of dems: Pelosi, Jerry Brown and the major or Berkeley.

Millions died to give the baby-boomers benefits they hated and despised.

Any kind of prominence brings haters.

They hate anything which has beauty, which elevates, which pleases or makes lives more enjoyable.

We have a savior, Jesus Christ. But there are also saviors of nations and this great leader is mine.

Thank God we finally have a real man at the helm.

FIGHT EVIL OR FIGHT STATUES?

Those who do not fight real evil fight statues.

You say you loved Obama, I say to hell with ya.

Deranged leftists think Trump is creating racist hurricanes.

Why seize guns after a hurricane--you mean we can't defend ourselves when we most need em?

Trump derangement syndrome is saying he caused Irma.

"Trump is a rapist so all supporters are accomplices to rape" Michael Moore

Trump was appointed by God for such a time as this: He's supported on high as we face the abyss.

SOLITUDE SOLUTION

Don't waste your precious breath on Joy Behar types. If these are your friends or family, yikes!

It's getting so you can't say anything. if it triggers, discomforts or even confuses them, you stink.

Crazy stupid women created by global media, public schools and no civics taught in schools.

Donald Trump is a massive relief and a breath of fresh air after all we've endured for eight terrible years.

They are sickening and getting more extreme after counseling with each other in their evil echo chambers.

All nations need good leaders and we've got the best. A great and noble man putting our interests first.

Our lethal enemy is stupidity. It prevents seeing and it's just like the master said we gotta forgive em.

Even Whoopi, Behar, that turncoat Bila, the whole mafia: no vision, forgive em.

The feminist mafia knows nothing but they still be railin' cuz it's about winning.

THE "VIEW" INTIMIDATES AS A GROUP

Ladies on The View can only intimidate as a group. Alone it's obvious they don't know the scoop.

Strong women acting like they need approval or acting out publicly with no control, I don't know...

Who the heck are they--The View--to criticize a great man like that? So arrogant to presume it, brats.

How can you take these silly women seriously, criticizing the great man Trump? They are nothing, crud.

They virtue signal (always), they act so arrogant in their "intelligence" and it's all just mimicry.

SOLITUDE SOLUTION

And to see weak women mimic Behar, take her views, even her arrogance and her petulance too.

Stiff-necked and haughty, self-involved and naughty. Lips curled up, gaudy.

They think alike, a true HERD. Superior man is independent, he is preferred.

True ladies can see the Godsent importance of Donald Trump. The rest are idiotic liberals, just crud.

It's too late, they will never see. All we can do is dig in/board up for when they come for you and me.

They give criminal illegals sanctuary with no thought of our safety, like we're inferior--yes, not maybe.

You'll hear all kinds of stories about Trump and none of it is true. They're so jealous of him, too.

Cultural Marxism is destruction of unique history and substituting a bland cartoon ideology.

If you say "all lives matter" you're attacked for being "racists"--only black matters to the fascists.

Living this way (in constant fear and preparedness for disaster) you're at your most intense, yes sir.

We gave up all hope after 8 years with a dope putting us on a dangerous and slippery slope.

They wanna make Donald look bad! What pathetic jokes as they put down the King, but we're glad.

LIBERALS AND THEIR MAKE BELIEVE WORLD

Liberals live in a make believe world. It's all a facade of mutual harmony but it's godless, girls.

SOLITUDE SOLUTION

The only one. You're a fool to vote for any one else--we'll be restored, we'll finally have fun.

FOX News stacked the commentators against Trump! That settles it--we're done with these skunks.

We've been so mad every day and thought we could do nothing but now through Trump there is hope/no bluffing.

I sense he's sincere, a breath of fresh air after 8 years of despair. People know, it's an air.

They wanna make Donald look bad--like a bloated capitalist idiot. Be ready for attacks from nitwits.

We've got to believe in somebody again. We all saw our doom sealed, no one cared even friends.

Donald says our leaders are incredibly stupid--what a breath of fresh air. Logic returned, I do declare!

Look at the government's bad deals--Trump is the only one with this art. Logic returned with heart.

We need a good capitalist--someone who knows about money. Not a cultural Marxist who is loony.

Trump didn't attack McCain enough cuz he wants to take our guns--needs to be more tough.

Mr. McCain may be a war hero but he wants victim disarmament. That's us, the unfortunate.

McCain wanted open borders and to take our guns. He threw us crumbs but Donald was the one.

PURITANS BROUGHT ORDER AND DISCIPLINE

Our Puritan beginnings made us a nation of order and discipline: people getting ahead with vision.

SOLITUDE SOLUTION

We don't wanna hear about anyone but Donald--ok? So stop with the other detractors--they're passe.

Cain's a war hero, captured and all the rest. But he still wants our guns and to allow in the un-best.

Donald we love your conceit. You can be as arrogant as you please having the strength of a fleet.

After all we've been through with you-know-who we see a light filled with fight showing God is true.

Christian families are very happy. The left wants to ruin that with immorality, making things crappy.

We can still come back and overcome the influence of Barrack: We can go to a castle from a shack.

The white man is under attack. A lot more than any of you know--by race you'll be tracked.

He makes us so happy, relieving frustration after such PC crap. We love Donald, even his spats.

Why aren't feminists against Islam and the way it treats women? Hah--they even love it, man.

Under Sharia women are stoned even if innocent victims. But feminists don't complain--just listen.

LIBERAL CONFORMISTS CONDONE IT ALL

The liberal conformists will go along with anything. They're in perfect unison changing with the wind.

Donald is the only one who can straighten this out. All the others are wimps-- they just have no clout.

So all whites are to blame but when radical muslims do something you don't even mention it, lame.

SOLITUDE SOLUTION

It's not only government demoting the white man but also the wife--he's worried about his very life.

Pray every day to be protected from your government. It's really come to this, maybe permanent.

It hurts being ostracized but that's how liberals play: mind what you say or it's a very bad day.

By them appeasing our deadly enemies it's the height of ignorant weakness and they can see it.

Donald is a light in the maize. The huge global corporate fraud that he's hep to--I'm dazed, so amazed.

Donald is the only one speaking to our troubles. The others are astounded as his popularity doubles.

Get away from cities, 250 miles from crowds. That's where the trouble is and they're so loud.

They will make you think like them and stop at nothing to do it. This is tyranny by trendies/the affluent.

FREEDOM-LOVING IS HOME-LOVING

Communist regimes are the most classist, racist and xenophobic contrary to their image magic.

They were so autocratic in the way they came at me for being a white racist without evidence.

Socialism is lowering your dreams of personal prosperity and taking crumbs off the table see.

1950-2010: student growth 100%, teacher growth 200% and administrative growth 800%!

There's nothing sexier than a freedom-loving woman but that's home-loving, what they're forbidding.

SOLITUDE SOLUTION

I don't care what you do in your bedroom--I don't want you teaching the kids to do what dooms.

Iran doesn't do deals with infidels so they'll do a deal for their own interest but ignore all the details.

Please Donald, do not disappoint. For we're sick of deception and have come to a turning point.

All men would be totally depraved were it not for God. it's like the default setting--being flawed.

Progressives want NO borders, they think it's good. But we're losing our ways and livelihoods.

Iran was such a bad deal it just makes me sick. We had far more power before--what finks.

It was such a bad deal--we gave it all away. What a laughing stock we are in the world today.

It was such a bad deal for us, not for them. We gave everything away--all our leverage too, gone.

I love *legal* immigration--I think it's wonderful. People must do the work to come here and make it legal.

People who condone illegal immigration are enemies cuz we're being killed in 300 sanctuary cities.

Liberals wanna let em all in--do they ever think of what it's doing to small towns, my friends?

Cloward and Piven: They're gonna let in the masses, all on the dole--then pull the plug now.

We can't let em organize. They may disagree with us then talk to each other. History, tyranny

I didn't want em to know I'm Jewish let alone German. I wanted to forget the whole thing. Ellen Brandt

KAREN KELLOCK PH.D.

M.S. Political Science, San Diego State. Ph.D. in Psychology, University of California Irvine. Postdoctoral: UCI School of Medicine, Dept. of Psychiatry [NIMH Grants]. Developed the Debris Theory of Disease, a theory of system pathology in 120 books and 22 textbooks for the general public. The theory has a general formula: All disease is obstruction, all recovery is elimination, all success is attraction. The three obstructions are people, habit and food. Remove obstruction and snap to your goals, waiting in the wings.

www.ingramcontent.com/pod-product-compliance
Lightning Source LLC
Chambersburg PA
CBHW061715250726
48657CB00002B/627